P9-CBT-567

UNDYING WORDS

1858–1865

OLIVIA MAHONEY
and JAMES CORNELIUS

Undying Words is generously sponsored in part by
Archer Daniels Midland Company

The exhibition *Undying Words: Lincoln, 1858–1865*
opened on November 20, 2014 at the Abraham Lincoln Presidential
Library and Museum.

Published in the United States of America in 2014 by the Illinois Historic
Preservation Agency.

© 2014 by the Illinois Historic Preservation Agency

All rights reserved.

No part of this publication may be reproduced in any manner whatsoever
without permission in writing of the Illinois Historic Preservation Agency.

ISBN 978-0-942579-07-9

Director: Amy Martin

Edited by Claudia Lamm Wood
Designed by Eileen Wagner Design, Inc.
Printed by: Bloomington Offset Printing, Inc.

Printed by the Authority of the State of Illinois   10/14   7M
Not paid for at taxpayer expense.

page iv: Inkwell used by Abraham Lincoln to write the First Inaugural Address,
ca. 1860. *ALPLM*

CONTENTS

TO MY SONS, ANDREW AND THOMAS BOULEANU
AND THE RADICAL CONCEPT OF HUMAN EQUALITY
—OM

TO ALL THOSE WHO PRESERVE AND LEARN FROM LINCOLN
—JMC

FOREWORD

*By Amy Martin, Executive Director of the Illinois Historic Preservation Agency
and Gary T. Johnson, President of the Chicago History Museum*

April 2015 marks the 150th anniversary of the Union victory in the Civil War and of Abraham Lincoln's assassination, as well as the tenth anniversary of the Abraham Lincoln Presidential Library and Museum. These anniversaries demand something special to mark the occasion, prompting the Presidential Library to develop a major new exhibition, *Undying Words: Lincoln, 1858–1865.*

The exhibition traces Lincoln's evolving views on slavery and racial equality through five key speeches that he delivered between 1858 and 1865. Lincoln's powerful words expressed an inner transformation that ultimately saved the nation and moved it closer to its founding ideals of human freedom and equality.

To deliver a truly extraordinary exhibition, the ALPLM teamed with the Chicago History Museum. Each of these institutions has a long connection to Lincoln's legacy. The Chicago History Museum was formed in 1856 as the Chicago Historical Society in the law office of J. Young Scammon, a close associate of Lincoln. In fact, Lincoln became an Honorary Member of the society. The Chicago History Museum today has one of the most significant Lincoln collections.

The Abraham Lincoln Presidential Library and Museum, created ten years ago by combining a new museum with the Illinois State Historical Library, draws on the state's 125 years of collecting Lincoln materials. The library's collection of Lincoln documents, artifacts, books, and art is now the largest in the world.

The new exhibition is the latest chapter in a long and productive story of cooperation. The Chicago History Museum loaned the Lincoln death bed for the opening of the Abraham Lincoln Presidential Library and Museum, and now, ten years later, it has returned. The presidential library in turn has been able to lend two of its most revered documents, the Emancipation Proclamation and the Gettysburg Address, for special exhibitions at the Chicago History Museum.

Between them, the two institutions have access to documents and artifacts that illustrate every part of Lincoln's life. The foremost difficulty in mounting this exhibition was sharpening the focus. An overview of Lincoln's life would be too general and probably overly familiar to most visitors; focusing on a particular event might shortchange the incredible breadth of his legacy. Ultimately, the curators decided to build the exhibition around Lincoln's ideas and words that still challenge and inspire people everywhere.

Undying Words would not have been possible without unfailing commitment to the educational value of Lincoln's legacy on the part of Governor Pat Quinn and the Board of Trustees of the Illinois Historic Preservation Agency, chaired by Sunny Fischer. We also owe a great debt of gratitude to the Abraham Lincoln Presidential Library Foundation, chaired by Wayne W. Whalen, and to the members of the many organizations in Illinois that are dedicated to the proposition that learning more about Lincoln is the very best form of civic education.

Many, many others also deserve thanks for their hard work.

The exhibition was curated by Olivia Mahoney of the Chicago History Museum and James Cornelius of the ALPLM.

Anna Margaret Barris, assisted by Clare Thorpe, oversaw the project for the Illinois Historic Preservation Agency.

We hope this exhibition reveals the full meaning and power of these truly undying words.

CURATORS' NOTES

Every exhibition is a collaborative endeavor, but this one required an extra level of cooperation and coordination between two separate institutions in different parts of the state. Many people deserve our thanks, but above all we must acknowledge Amy Martin, Director of the Illinois Historic Preservation Agency, who enthusiastically launched the project and successfully guided our efforts to completion. Gary T. Johnson, President of the Chicago History Museum, embraced the collaboration and generously agreed to lend several key pieces to the exhibition. We would also like to thank Sunny Fischer, chair of the Illinois Historic Preservation Agency board of trustees, for encouraging us to explore Lincoln's ideas in an exhibition format.

We are especially indebted to Amy Reichert, exhibition designer, and her assistant, Jason Mould, for creating a thoughtful, engaging, and accessible installation for museum visitors. Claudia Lamm Wood masterfully edited the exhibition labels and catalog essay, and also managed the production of the catalog. Eileen Wagner designed the catalog with great care and sensitivity to the subject. We are also grateful to Eric Foner, DeWitt Clinton Professor of History at Columbia University, for reviewing the labels and catalog essay. His corrections and helpful suggestions improved our efforts immeasurably. Special thanks also go to Michael Mahoney for reading the first draft of the catalog essay.

The exhibition would not have been possible without a team of dedicated professionals at both institutions. ALPLM staff members included Carla Smith, registrar; Mike Casey, exhibition fabricator; Bonnie Parr, conservator; Jennifer Ericson, Lincoln images; Mary Ann Pohl, Lincoln cataloger; Clare Thorpe, guest services; Phil Funkenbusch, theater director; and Sam Cooper, technical director for image projections. In addition, Anna Margaret Barris, special assistant to Director Martin, and Kristy Bond, marketing director of the Illinois Historic Preservation Agency, provided critical assistance throughout the project.

CHM staff included Julie Katz, registrar; Jamie Lewis, registration technician; Holly Lundberg and Carol Turchan, conservators; Christine McNulty, collection manager; Joseph Campbell and Stephen Jensen, photographers; Angela Hoover and Jessica Herczeg-Konecny, licensing and reproductions coordinators; and Alison Eisendrath, Andrew W. Mellon director of collection services. John Russick, director of curatorial affairs, and Russell Lewis, executive vice president and chief historian, provided critical feedback on the exhibition storyline and labels, as well as the catalog manuscript. Finally, we would like to thank our families for their support and encouragement throughout the project.

Olivia Mahoney, Senior Curator, Chicago History Museum

James M. Cornelius, Lincoln Curator, Abraham Lincoln Presidential Library and Museum

Abraham Lincoln, September 26, 1858. Photograph by C.S. German, Springfield, Illinois. *ALPLM*
Facing page, backdrop: First printing of "A House Divided" speech, 1858 (detail). *ALPLM*

CHAPTER I

A HOUSE DIVIDED

We are now far into the *fifth* year, since a policy was initiated with the *avowed* object, and *confident* promise, of putting an end to slavery agitation.

Under the operation of that policy, that agitation has not only *not ceased*, but has constantly augmented.

In *my* opinion, it *will* not cease, until a crisis shall have been reached, and passed.

" A house divided against itself cannot stand."

I believe this Government cannot endure, permanently, half *slave* and half *free*.

I do not expect the Union to be *dissolved* —I don't expect the house to *fall*—but I *do* expect it will cease to be divided.

It will become *all* one thing, or *all* the other.

Either the *opponents* of slavery will arrest the further spread of it, and place it where the public mind shall rest in the belief that it is in course of ultimate extinction ; or it

"A HOUSE DIVIDED AGAINST ITSELF CANNOT STAND. I BELIEVE THIS GOVERNMENT CANNOT ENDURE, PERMANENTLY HALF *SLAVE* AND HALF *FREE*."

Lincoln spoke these memorable words on June 16, 1858. He had just been nominated by the Republican party for the U.S. Senate at their state convention in Springfield, Illinois. His acceptance speech kicked off a campaign to unseat the powerful Democratic incumbent, Stephen A. Douglas, by focusing on slavery, the era's most critical issue. The "House Divided" speech clearly reveals Lincoln's thinking in 1858 and, therefore, provides a useful starting point to explore how and why his views on slavery and racial equality changed over time.

In "House Divided," Lincoln argued that the Congress, the Supreme Court, and the current president, James Buchanan, were conspiring to make the United States a slave nation. The conspiracy, described by Lincoln as a "piece of machinery," resulted in the Kansas-Nebraska Act of 1854 and the Dred Scott decision of 1857. The "Nebraska Act," as Lincoln called it, opened western territories to slavery, where it had been previously barred by the Missouri Compromise of 1820. Written by Douglas, the act embodied the doctrine of popular sovereignty, allowing territorial settlers to vote for or against slavery. Its passage ignited a firestorm of controversy and triggered a bloody civil war in Kansas between proslavery and antislavery forces. In 1857, the Supreme Court ruled in the case of *Dred Scott v. Sandford* that African Americans, whether slave or free, could not be American citizens and therefore had no right to sue in federal court. The court also decreed that Congress had no authority to ban slavery from the western territories. Lincoln included Buchanan in the grand conspiracy because he supported the Supreme Court's controversial decision.

At the time of Lincoln's address, slavery occupied the center stage of American politics. Nearly four million African American slaves lived in the South, making the United States the largest slave-owning country in the history of the modern world. The first black slaves—twenty in number—arrived in 1619 in the English colony of Jamestown, Virginia. From that small beginning, slavery began to spread, slowly at first, then more rapidly to meet a growing demand for labor. Slavery existed in the northern colonies but primarily flourished in the South, where large plantations required many hands. As a result, North and South evolved into two distinct regions. A free labor system consisting of farmers, merchants, and businessmen characterized the North, while the South relied upon an extensive system of slave labor.

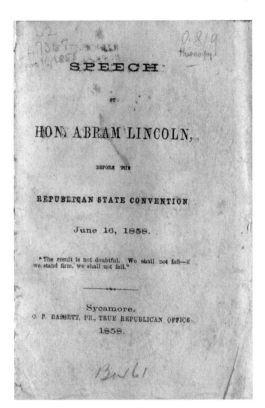

SPEECH

OF

HON. ABRAM LINCOLN,

BEFORE THE

REPUBLICAN STATE CONVENTION.

June 16, 1858.

"The result is not doubtful. We shall not fail—if we stand firm, we shall not fail."

Sycamore.
O. P. BASSETT, PR., TRUE REPUBLICAN OFFICE.
1858.

Lincoln's speech was widely circulated in newspapers and pamphlets, such as this first printing from Sycamore Illinois. Though powerful, Lincoln's speech avoided any mention of the human cost involved, despite the presence of nearly four million African Americans enslaved at the time. *Below*: Slave shackles, ca. 1855. *ALPLM, CHM*

COTTON PRESSING IN LOUISIANA

Slavery supported the Southern economy while aiding the nation's as well. This illustration depicts slaves baling cotton for sale to distant markets in the North and Europe. *CHM*

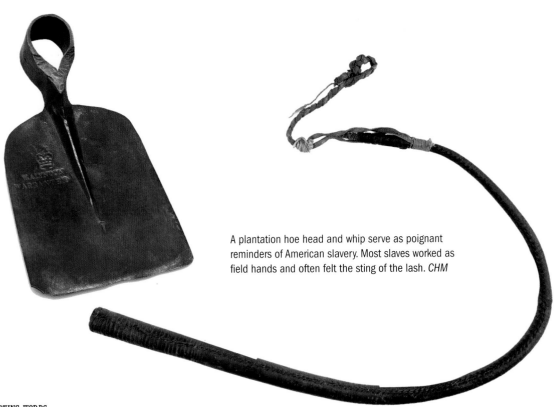

A plantation hoe head and whip serve as poignant reminders of American slavery. Most slaves worked as field hands and often felt the sting of the lash. *CHM*

Printed by the Anti-Slavery Society of Boston, this broadside proposes Northern secession from the slave-holding South, a view rejected by Lincoln who believed that the Union must be maintained at all cost. *CHM*

In the colonial era and through the first half of the nineteenth century, slavery permeated and shaped every aspect of Southern life. Cotton, rice, and tobacco grown by slaves were the region's chief exports. Slavery also fueled the national economy with cotton shipped to textile mills in the northeastern states or exported to England. Without mentioning the word, the U.S. Constitution protected slavery in Article I, Section III that provided for the counting of each slave as three-fifths of a person in determining Congressional representation. For the bondsman, slavery meant a life of unremitting toil and hardship. Most slaves worked as field hands or house servants on large plantations but others toiled as craftsmen in urban areas. Family members were frequently separated by sale and runaways were hunted down and severely punished, but, above all, slaves had neither personal freedom nor a chance to better themselves. As Frederick Douglass noted when recalling his desire for freedom, "My feelings were not the result of any marked cruelty in the treatment I received; they sprang from the consideration of my being a slave at all. It was slavery, not its mere incidents, that I hated."

The presence of slavery in a nation founded on the lofty ideals of human freedom and equality stirred a bitter political debate that, by 1850, threatened to tear the country apart. While its supporters claimed that the system benefited owners, slaves, and the entire nation, antislavery forces firmly disagreed. They considered slavery morally evil, and many called for its immediate end, or abolition. The abolitionist movement sprang up in the 1830s. Among its leaders were William Lloyd Garrison and Wendell Phillips, Boston abolitionists who were instrumental in establishing the American Anti-Slavery Society in 1833. They demanded an immediate end to slavery, endorsed equal

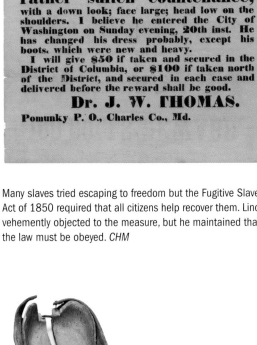

Sale of Slaves and Stock.

The Negroes and Stock listed below, are a Prime Lot, and belong to the ESTATE OF THE LATE LUTHER McGOWAN, and will be sold on Monday, Sept. 22nd, 1852, at the Fair Grounds, in Savannah, Georgia, at 1:00 P. M. The Negroes will be taken to the grounds two days previous to the Sale, so that they may be inspected by prospective buyers.

On account of the low prices listed below, they will be sold for cash only, and must be taken into custody within two hours after sale.

No.	Name.	Age.	Remarks.	Price.
1	Lunesta	27	Prime Rice Planter,	$1,275.00
2	Violet	16	Housework and Nursemaid,	900.00
3	Lizzie	30	Rice, Unsound,	300.00
4	Minda	27	Cotton, Prime Woman,	1,200.00
5	Adam	28	Cotton, Prime Young Man,	1,100.00
6	Abel	41	Rice Hand, Eyesight Poor,	675.00
7	Tanney	22	Prime Cotton Hand,	950.00
8	Flementina	39	Good Cook, Stiff Knee,	400.00
9	Lanney	34	Prime Cotton Man,	1,000.00
10	Sally	10	Handy in Kitchen,	675.00
11	Maccabey	35	Prime Man, Fair Carpenter,	980.00
12	Dorcas Judy	25	Seamstress, Handy in House.	800.00
13	Happy	60	Blacksmith,	575.00
14	Mowden	15	Prime Cotton Boy,	700.00
15	Bills	21	Handy with Mules,	900.00
16	Theopolis	39	Rice Hand, Gets Fits,	575.00
17	Coolidge	29	Rice Hand and Blacksmith,	1,275.00
18	Bessie	69	Infirm, Sews,	250.00
19	Infant	1	Strong Likely Boy	400.00
20	Samson	41	Prime Man, Good with Stock.	975.00
21	Callie May	27	Prime Woman, Rice,	1,000.00
22	Honey	14	Prime Girl, Hearing Poor,	850.00
23	Angelina	16	Prime Girl, House or Field,	1,000.00
24	Virgil	21	Prime Field Hand,	1,100.00
25	Tom	40	Rice Hand, Lame Leg,	750.00
26	Noble	11	Handy Boy.	900.00
27	Judge Lesh	55	Prime Blacksmith,	800.00
28	Booster	43	Fair Mason, Unsound,	600.00
29	Big Kate	37	Housekeeper and Nurse,	950.00
30	Melie Ann	19	Housework, Smart Yellow Girl,	1,250.00
31	Deacon	26	Prime Rice Hand,	1,000.00
32	Coming	19	Prime Cotton Hand,	1,000.00
33	Mabel	47	Prime Cotton Hand,	800.00
34	Uncle Tim	60	Fair Hand with Mules,	600.00
35	Abe	27	Prime Cotton Hand,	1,000.00
36	Tennes	29	Prime Rice Hand and Cocahman,	1,250.00

There will also be offered at this sale, twenty head of Horses and Mules with harness, along with thirty head of Prime Cattle. Slaves will be sold separate, or in lots, as best suits the purchaser. Sale will be held rain or shine.

100 DOLLS. REWARD.

RAN AWAY

From me, on Saturday, the 19th inst.,

Negro Boy Robert Porter,

aged 19; heavy, stoutly made; dark chesnut complexion; rather sullen countenance, with a down look; face large; head low on the shoulders. I believe he entered the City of Washington on Sunday evening, 20th inst. He has changed his dress probably, except his boots, which were new and heavy.

I will give $50 if taken and secured in the District of Columbia, or $100 if taken north of the District, and secured in each case and delivered before the reward shall be good.

Dr. J. W. THOMAS.

Pomunky P. O., Charles Co., Md.

Lincoln considered slavery morally evil but did not speak out against the buying and selling of human beings. As this broadside reveals, prime field hands and skilled craftsmen fetched the highest prices. *CHM*

Many slaves tried escaping to freedom but the Fugitive Slave Act of 1850 required that all citizens help recover them. Lincoln vehemently objected to the measure, but he maintained that the law must be obeyed. *CHM*

Lincoln believed that slaves had the right to be free and to improve their lives. This worn-out pair of shoes used by a field hand illustrates that they had neither. *CHM*

citizenship rights for blacks, and advocated separation from the South. By 1840, well over one hundred thousand Northerners had joined abolitionist societies. Women and free blacks played a key role, organizing meetings, publishing pamphlets, and delivering lectures. Abolitionists, however, remained a minority. Most Northerners accepted slavery's presence in the South but many opposed its westward expansion.

Lincoln thus struck a chord in "House Divided" when he said that the current situation "shows exactly where we now *are*; and *partially* also, whither we are tending." He predicted, "We shall lie *down* pleasantly dreaming that the people of *Missouri* are on the verge of making their State *free*; and we shall awake to the reality, instead, that the Supreme Court has made *Illinois* a slave *State*." This latter decision, he claimed, would logically follow from Dred Scott. To prevent such a calamity, Lincoln encouraged voters "to meet and overthrow the power of that dynasty" in the upcoming election by defeating Senator Douglas, the conspiracy's "*aptest* instrument."

Lincoln did not fully articulate his views on slavery in the speech but they informed every word. A political moderate, Lincoln occupied middle ground within the Republican Party, which had been founded two years earlier to oppose slavery's expansion. He considered slavery morally evil, and he believed it mocked America's democratic ideals while impeding the country's progress toward greatness. Lincoln believed that blacks, like whites, were entitled to the inalienable rights of "life, liberty and the pursuit of happiness" and that they should be paid for their labor, but he did not believe that blacks were socially or politically equal to whites.

Lincoln firmly opposed the western extension of slavery, believing instead that it should be contained in the South, where the archaic system would eventually die out on its own. Above all, Lincoln was not an abolitionist fearing such action would have revolutionary consequences. Instead, Lincoln proposed gradual, compensated emancipation, a process that would take generations and millions of dollars in monetary compensation paid to Southern slaveholders. Finally, Lincoln did not believe that blacks and whites could live together peacefully, and he endorsed a system of voluntary colonization of freed blacks to Africa, where they could advance on their own.

Lincoln's views on slavery were shaped during his early life and public career. He was born in Kentucky, a slave state, and later moved with his family to the free states of Indiana and Illinois. He grew up in a farm family of modest means but set his own course in life by pursuing a successful career in politics and law. A long-time member of the Whig Party, Lincoln served in the Illinois state legislature from 1834 to 1842. In 1846, he won a seat in the U.S. House of Representatives, but he served only a single term of two years before returning home to Springfield, where he concentrated his energies on practicing law to support a growing family.

Lincoln's strong performance in the Great Debates with Douglas made him a national figure. This portrait is by William Camm, an English immigrant artist who met Lincoln at a campaign stop during the summer of 1858. *ALPLM*

At the time of the Great Debates, Democratic Senator Stephen A. Douglas of Illinois was the most powerful politician in America. This portrait by Louis Lussier, a Canadian-born artist, skillfully captures the "Little Giant." *CHM*

In this note, dated July 31, 1858, Lincoln agrees to giving Douglas four openings to his three in the upcoming debates. Lincoln also suggests publishing their correspondence in the Springfield newspapers for added publicity. *CHM*

Lincoln's brief set of notes for the Jonesboro debate concludes with a key question: "Can the people of a United States Territory, in any lawful way . . . exclude slavery . . . prior to the formation of a State Constitution?" *ALPLM*

Lincoln's true passion, however, remained politics. After Congress passed the Kansas-Nebraska Act in 1854, Lincoln decided to run for the Illinois state legislature as an antislavery candidate. A series of powerful speeches in Bloomington, Springfield, and Peoria helped Lincoln win the election, but he quickly resigned his seat to present himself as a candidate for the U.S. Senate, at a time when the legislature chose senators. He lost his bid as well as his party when the Whigs collapsed over the slavery issue. In 1856, Lincoln joined the newly formed Republican Party, which opposed the extension of slavery while promoting the free labor system of Northern farmers and businessmen. Lincoln strove to establish the party in Illinois and actively campaigned for its first presidential candidate, John C. Frémont. In June 1858, Illinois Republican leaders rewarded Lincoln's efforts by nominating him to run against Douglas for the U.S. Senate.

COLONIZATION

Colonization was Lincoln's most controversial idea but one he shared with many people. Indeed, Lincoln adopted the views of Henry Clay, his political idol, in this regard. Clay (1777–1852), a wealthy Kentuckian, served as secretary of state, member and speaker of the U.S. House of Representatives, and U.S. senator. He helped found the Whig Party and ran for president three times. Although a slaveholder, Clay disliked the system's divisive effects on the country and proposed a plan of gradual, compensated emancipation. He did not ever believe that blacks and whites could live peacefully together and helped found the American Colonization Society (ACS) in 1816 to move free blacks to Africa where they could advance on their own. Its large membership included African Americans who believed that they would never have racial justice in America. In 1822, the ACS established a colony on the west coast of Africa that became the independent nation of Liberia in 1847.

In his eulogy for Clay in 1852, Lincoln praised colonization as "the possible redemption of the African race and the African people. . . . May it indeed be realized!" The following year, Lincoln addressed a Springfield colonization society and the state society in 1855; two years later, the state society elected Lincoln as one of its managers. Lincoln discussed colonization in his first debate with Stephen Douglas at Ottawa by quoting from a speech he made at Peoria in 1854. "'If all earthly power were given me,'" he said, "'I should not know what to do, as to the existing institution. My first impulse would be to free all the slaves, and send them to Liberia,—to their own native land—But a moment's reflection would convince me, that whatever of high hope, (as I think there is) there may be in this, in the long run, its sudden execution is impossible.'" Lincoln continued to promote colonization well into his presidency but finally abandoned the idea after issuing the Emancipation Proclamation.

Henry Clay, engraving by John Sartain, 1861, from a painting by M. A. Root. *ALPLM*

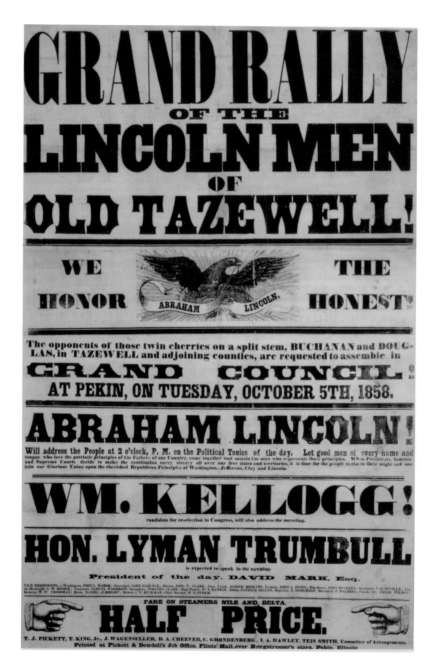

A festive poster announcing Lincoln's appearance at a campaign rally in Pekin also proclaims that Illinois congressmen William Kellogg and Lyman Trumbull would be in attendance. Note Lincoln's speaking time of two o'clock. *ALPLM*

Lincoln campaigned hard for the position, starting with his "House Divided" acceptance speech in Springfield, followed by a rousing address in Chicago on July 10. Lincoln spoke that evening from the balcony of the Tremont House, a popular hotel in the downtown district. The night before, Douglas had spoken from the same balcony, offering a spirited defense of his Kansas-Nebraska Act. Lincoln took his turn with an equally vigorous attack on Douglas, popular sovereignty, and the Dred Scott decision. Lincoln expanded upon the themes of his "House Divided" speech and added a critical personal comment by stating, "I have always hated slavery, I think as much as any Abolitionist." Though not an abolitionist, Lincoln knew his audience, as Chicago supported a small but active cadre of abolitionists, many of whom attended Lincoln's speech.

The candidates' back-to-back appearances in Chicago drew huge crowds and led to a series of debates later that summer and early fall. Lincoln and Douglas crisscrossed the state to engage in seven debates that attracted national attention. The candidates stood in sharp physical contrast. Nearly six feet four inches tall, Lincoln towered over the "Little Giant," a full foot shorter. Lincoln wore an ill-fitting, rumpled black suit and had a high-pitched speaking voice with a nasal twang. His more sophisticated opponent wore a fashionable white suit and was an accomplished orator, the result of giving thousands of public addresses during his long career. The candidates expressed stark political differences, too. While Lincoln firmly opposed the western extension of slavery, Douglas argued that settlers had the right to decide the issue for themselves. Lincoln called slavery a great evil while Douglas insisted that the people of each state or territory should decide moral issues for themselves.

Throughout the debates, Douglas persistently charged Lincoln with being an abolitionist who wanted to bring about full equality between blacks and whites, a radical position that would have alienated many voters. Lincoln responded by denying that he favored equal civil or political rights for blacks, but he insisted that all persons were entitled to the inalienable rights—life, liberty, and the pursuit of happiness—identified in the Declaration of Independence. Although Lincoln lost the election to Douglas, his skillful performance in the Great Debates, as they became known, made him a rising star of American politics.

Despite his loss, Lincoln remained active in politics. He continued speaking against slavery in 1859 in addresses in Chicago, Columbus, and Cincinnati, followed by a triumphant speech at the Cooper Institute, New York, on February 27, 1860, in which he argued that the founding fathers intended for slavery to remain confined to the South and not spread into other regions of the country. Lincoln's efforts prompted others to mention him as a potential candidate for the 1860 Republican presidential nomination. He tried to downplay the attention but confessed to his friend and fellow Republican, U.S. Senator Lyman Trumbull of Illinois, "I will be entirely frank. The taste *is* in my mouth a little."

President-elect Abraham Lincoln, February 9, 1861. Photograph by C. S. German, Springfield, Illinois. *ALPLM*
Facing page, backdrop: Printer's galleys of Lincoln's First Inaugural Address, 1861 (detail). *ALPLM*

CHAPTER 2

THE FIRST INAUGURAL ADDRESS

"I HAVE NO PURPOSE . . . TO INTERFERE WITH THE INSTITUTION OF SLAVERY IN THE STATES WHERE IT EXISTS."

On March 4, 1861, Abraham Lincoln, age fifty-two, took office as sixteenth president of the United States. He had defeated three other candidates the previous November 4 in a contentious election centered on the slavery issue. Lincoln was the first Republican to win the presidency, a cause of great celebration throughout the North. But his victory triggered a grave crisis. Within weeks South Carolina seceded from the Union. Six other states quickly followed, fearing that Lincoln would interfere with slavery inside their borders. In swift order, they formed the Confederate States of America, adopted a constitution, and installed a president, former senator Jefferson Davis of Mississippi. As Lincoln said when departing Springfield for his inaugural ceremony, he faced "a task . . . greater than that which rested upon Washington."

Indeed, Southern secession confirmed what many observers had predicted for the world's only democracy—failure. But Lincoln responded to the crisis with a carefully worded address aimed at peacefully wooing back the South while expressing a firm resolve to save the Union. Lincoln spoke from the east side of the U.S. Capitol building to a large crowd of about twenty-five thousand people. Seated behind Lincoln were three men he had named in his landmark "House Divided" speech as participants in a national conspiracy to make the United States a slave nation: outgoing president James R. Buchanan; Democratic senator Stephen A. Douglas; and Supreme Court justice Roger B. Taney, who would administer the oath of office to Lincoln.

Lincoln opened his address by recalling tradition. "In compliance with a custom as old as the government itself, I appear before you to address you briefly, and to take, in your presence, the oath prescribed by the Constitution of the United States." Lincoln then tackled the issue of secession head on: "Apprehension seems to exist among the people of the Southern States, that by the accession of a Republican Administration, their property [slaves] and their peace, and personal security are to be endangered." Lincoln denied any such intention, stating that proof "is found in nearly all the published speeches of him who now addresses you." He followed, "I do but quote from one of those speeches when I declare that 'I have no purpose, directly or indirectly, to interfere with the institution of slavery in the States where it exists. I believe I have no lawful right to do so, and I have no inclination to do so.'" To underscore his point, Lincoln added, "Those who nominated and

Displayed at campaign rallies, *The Railsplitter* portrays Lincoln as a self-reliant frontiersman on his way to the White House, shimmering in the distance. The imagery appealed to many Northern voters with similar backgrounds and cultural values. *CHM*

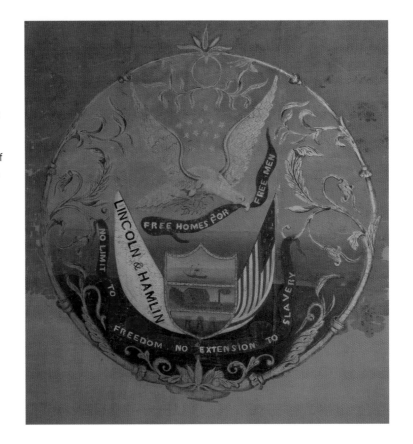

A colorful silk banner from 1860 expresses the Republican Party platform that opposed the western extension of slavery. Notice Lincoln's name paired with that of his running mate, Senator Hannibal Hamlin of Maine. *ALPLM*

elected me did so with full knowledge that I had made this, and many similar declarations, and had never recanted them." Moreover, he ran on a platform that vowed to respect "the right of each State to order and control its own domestic institutions . . . and denounce the lawless invasion by armed force of the soil of any State or Territory, no matter under what pretext, as among the gravest of crimes."

Lincoln followed by raising the issue of fugitive slaves, about which "there is much controversy." Southerners feared a Republican Congress would repeal the Fugitive Slave Act of 1850 that made assisting runaway slaves a federal crime and their return mandatory under financial penalty. Lincoln reassured Southerners that "All members of Congress swear their support to the whole Constitution—to this provision as much as to any other." He stated that he, too, was bound to support the Constitution: "I take the official oath to-day, with no mental reservations, and with no purpose to construe the Constitution or laws." Yet he also suggested changes in the law to ensure that free blacks were not sent to the South as slaves under its provisions, suggestions that were unlikely to reassure the South.

Having addressed Southern fears about slavery, Lincoln moved on to the "disruption of the Federal Union," in other words, secession. Here, Lincoln argued that the Union was inviolable:

> I hold, that in contemplation of universal law, and of the Constitution, the Union of these States is perpetual. Perpetuity is implied, if not expressed, in the fundamental law of all national governments. It is safe to assert that no government proper, ever had a provision in its organic law for its own termination.

Even if, Lincoln argued, the United States was not a proper government but an association of states in the nature of a contract, can a contract "be peaceably unmade, by less than all the parties who made it? One party . . . may violate it . . . but does it not require all to lawfully rescind it?"

Lincoln drew a lawyerly conclusion. "Descending from these general principles, we find the proposition, the Union is perpetual, confirmed by the history of the Union itself." Indeed, "The Union is much older than the Constitution . . . formed in fact, by the Articles of Association in 1774 . . . matured and continued by the Declaration of Independence in 1776 . . . further matured . . . by the Articles of Confederation in 1778," and made "more perfect" by the Constitution in 1787. In Lincoln's view, the founding fathers established the Union to protect the basic human right "to life, liberty, and the pursuit of happiness." The Union, therefore, held a higher moral purpose than other nations.

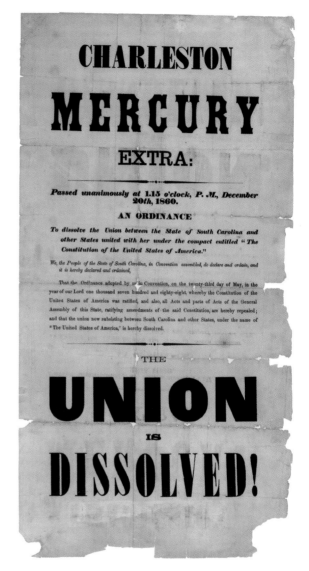

Six weeks after Lincoln's election to the presidency, South Carolina seceded from the Union. They made their intentions clear in this broadside, printed by the *Charleston Mercury* on December 20, 1860. *ALPLM*

LINCOLN'S WHITE HOUSE

Abraham Lincoln assumed the presidency with little experience at the national level, but he appointed an experienced team of leaders to his original cabinet. They included Lincoln's chief rivals for the Republican nomination: Senator William H. Seward of New York as secretary of state, Senator Salmon P. Chase of Ohio as secretary of the treasury, and Edward Bates of Missouri as attorney general. Additional appointments included Simon Cameron as secretary of war, later replaced with Edwin M. Stanton, Gideon Welles as secretary of the navy, and Montgomery Blair as postmaster general. Hannibal Hamlin, former senator from Maine, served as vice president while two personal secretaries, John Nicolay and John Hay, provided loyal support.

Throughout the war, Lincoln lived at the White House (then called the Executive Mansion) with his wife, Mary, and two of their three sons, William (Willie) and Thomas (Tad). Their eldest son, Robert, was away most of the time, studying at Harvard University. Early in the administration, scandal erupted over Mary's lavish spending on redecorating and entertaining during wartime. Her Kentucky background and numerous family ties to members of the Confederate army led to widespread suspicion that she was a Southern sympathizer or, worse, a spy. Willie's tragic death in 1862 sent both parents into deep mourning from which Mary never fully recovered. The family's personal staff included two African Americans: William H. Johnson, a free black and Lincoln's personal valet from Springfield, and Elizabeth H. Keckly, a former slave who served as Mary's seamstress and confidante.

En route to his inauguration, Lincoln purchased this carriage in New York City for his family's use in Washington, D.C. The vehicle's simple yet elegant appearance is suited to the president of a people's republic rather than a member of European royalty. *CHM*

(left) The Lincolns' eldest son, Robert, attended Harvard and didn't spend much time with his family at the White House. Mathew Brady took Robert's portrait in 1861, shortly after his father assumed office. *ALPLM*

(center) The death of young Willie Lincoln sent both parents into deep mourning, but while Mary wept openly, Lincoln grieved alone. This 1862 watercolor portrait by an unknown artist is based on a Mathew Brady photograph. *ALPLM*

(right) Mary Todd Lincoln, photographed by Mathew Brady in 1861, supported her husband's political career but experienced both public controversy and personal tragedy as First Lady. *ALPLM*

Lincoln continued by saying, "no State, upon its own mere motion, can lawfully get out of the Union," and that such acts are "insurrectionary or revolutionary." Conversely, Southern secessionists believed that states held greater authority than the Union and that they could leave at any time. But Lincoln refused to acknowledge secession as a legal act, "I therefore consider that . . . the Union is unbroken." Lincoln continued that he, as president, would "take care . . . that the laws of the Union be faithfully executed in all the States" and that the Union "*will* constitutionally defend, and maintain itself." But, in doing so, "there needs to be no bloodshed or violence, unless it be forced upon the national authority." He vowed that beyond what was necessary to protect and preserve federal property, there would be "no invasion—no using of force against, or among the people anywhere." At this point, Lincoln was willing to let the South return with slavery intact, a position in keeping with his long-held views.

Lincoln admitted that there were "persons in one section, or another who seek to destroy the Union at all events" but he wanted to address those "who really love the Union" to "ascertain" why they seceded. Lincoln identified the reasons as agitation over the fugitive slave law and extension of slavery, and he pointed out that the Constitution

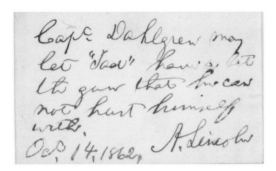

Capt. Dahlgren may
let "Tad" have a little
gun that he can
not hurt himself
with.
Oct. 14, 1862.   A. Lincoln

Thomas or "Tad," the Lincolns' youngest son, wears a light summer suit in this rare, hand-colored photograph taken in 1861 and attributed to Mathew Brady. At the time, Tad was eight years old. *ALPLM*

At Lincoln's request, Captain John A. Dahlgren gave Tad this model of a naval cannon. Lincoln asked for "a little gun that he can not hurt himself with" and Dahlgren obligingly bent the firing pin. *ALPLM*

does not say anything about prohibiting or protecting slavery in the territories. Yet, from those questions "spring all our . . . controversies and we divide upon them into majorities and minorities." If the minority, however, secedes rather than acquiesce in majority rule, they set a precedent for further secession, the central idea of which Lincoln deemed to be "the essence of anarchy." And, he continued, the rule of a minority, "as a permanent arrangement, is wholly inadmissible; so that, rejecting the majority principle, anarchy, or despotism in some form, is all that is left."

Lincoln then appealed directly to the South. "In your hands, my dissatisfied fellow countrymen, and not in mine, is the momentous issue of civil war." He made a pointed reminder that they had "no oath registered in Heaven to destroy the government" while he would take a "most solemn one to 'preserve, protect and defend' it." Lincoln closed his speech with what became its most famous passage, an eloquent plea for reconciliation:

> *"I am loth to close. We are not enemies, but friends. We must not be enemies. Though passion may have strained, it must not break the bonds of affection. The mystic chords of memory, stretching from every battle-field and patriot grave, to every living heart and hearthstone, all over this broad land will yet swell the chorus of Union, when again touched, as surely they will be, by the better angels of our nature."*

Lincoln's words fell on deaf ears. Six weeks later, on April 12, 1861, Confederate forces opened fire on Fort Sumter in Charleston Harbor. It fell two days later and Lincoln called for twelve thousand volunteers to "put down the rebellion." The Civil War had begun.

As depicted in a popular print by Currier & Ives, the Civil War began in the early morning hours of April 12, 1861, with a ferocious rebel attack on Fort Sumter. *CHM*

Abraham Lincoln, November 8, 1863. Photograph by Alexander Gardner, Washington, D.C. *ALPLM*
Facing page, backdrop: Gettysburg Address, by Abraham Lincoln (detail). *ALPLM*

CHAPTER 3
THE GETTYSBURG ADDRESS

"FOUR SCORE AND SEVEN YEARS AGO, OUR FATHERS BROUGHT FORTH ON THIS CONTINENT, A NEW NATION, CONCEIVED IN LIBERTY, AND DEDICATED TO THE PROPOSITION THAT ALL MEN ARE CREATED EQUAL."

On November 19, 1863, Abraham Lincoln spoke at the dedication of a new military cemetery at Gettysburg, Pennsylvania, site of the war's greatest battle. About twenty thousand people came to hear the president speak that day. He had not spoken publicly since his inauguration in March 1861 and much had changed since then. After two years of military setbacks and failures, Union forces finally seemed to be gaining the upper hand. They achieved major victories at Gettysburg and Vicksburg the previous July, and slavery was crumbling as well. The Civil War was sweeping away the old order while creating a new and unfamiliar world.

Yet Lincoln did not begin his brief address (it lasted only two minutes) with an update on the war but, rather, with an eloquent reminder that, "Four score and seven years ago, our fathers brought forth on this continent, a new nation, conceived in Liberty, and dedicated to the proposition that all men are created equal." Lincoln considered the Declaration of Independence to be America's founding document, a belief he had advanced in many previous speeches. "Now," he continued, "we are engaged in a great civil war, testing whether that nation, or any nation so conceived and so dedicated, can long endure." The war certainly tested the nation as the conflict grew larger, costlier, and deadlier than anyone could have predicted when it began. But the war also tested Lincoln, who vividly described the conflict as "the fiery trial through which we pass."

Lincoln's crucible occurred in 1862 when a critical convergence of personal loss, military defeat, and political failure forced him to reexamine and ultimately abandon his old ideas about slavery in favor of a new way to save the Union. Lincoln's trials began with the tragic death of his eleven-year-old son, Willie, on February 20, 1862. Mary Lincoln grieved openly but Lincoln, an intensely private man, shut himself up in his room to weep alone. The loss of another child (Edward, age three, had died in 1850) had a profound effect on Lincoln. Though not a regular churchgoer, Lincoln sought spiritual comfort from his Washington pastor, the Reverend Phineas D. Gurley, and he said later that he experienced "a process of crystallization" in his religious beliefs. Lincoln's personal crisis, followed by what seems to have been a spiritual awakening, coincided with some of the war's darkest moments and may have encouraged him to seek a new direction in earthly matters as well.

Four score and seven years ago our fathers brought forth upon this continent, a new nation, conceived in Liberty, and dedicated to the proposition that all men are created equal.

Now we are engaged in a great civil war, testing whether that nation, or any nation so conceived, and so dedicated, can long endure. We are met on a great battle-field of that war. We have come to dedicate a portion of that field, as a final resting place for those who here gave their lives, that that nation might live. It is altogether fitting and proper that we should do this.

But, in a larger sense, we can not dedicate— we can not consecrate— we can not hallow— this ground. The brave men, living and dead, who struggled here, have consecrated it, far above our poor power to add or detract. The world will little note, nor long remember, what we say here, but it can never forget what they did here. It is for us, the living, rather, to be dedicated here to the unfinished work which they, who fought here, have, thus far, so nobly advanced. It is rather for us to be here dedicated to the great task remaining before us— that from these honored dead we take increased devotion to that cause for which they here gave the last full measure of devotion— that we here highly resolve that these dead shall not have died in vain— that this nation, under God, shall have a new birth of freedom— and that government of the people, by the people, for the people, shall not perish from the earth.

This is one of five known copies of the Gettysburg Address. Lincoln made it for Edward Everett, a noted orator who spoke first and at much greater length at Gettysburg. It was the first copy to include the words "under God." Everett sold both of their speeches for $10,000 at the New York Sanitary Fair in April 1864 to benefit sick and wounded Union army soldiers. *ALPLM*

Executive Mansion
Washington, March 11. 1862.

President's War
Orders, No. 3

    Major General McClellan having personally taken the field at the head of the Army of the Potomac, until otherwise ordered, he is relieved from the command of the other Military departments, he retaining command of the Department of the Potomac—

    Ordered further that the two departments now under the respective commands of Generals Halleck and Hunter be consolidated, and designated the Department of the Mississippi; and that, until otherwise ordered, Major General Halleck have command of said department.

    Ordered also, that the country West of the Department of the Potomac and East of the Department of the Mississippi, be a Military department to be called the Mountain Department, and that the same be commanded by Major General Fremont.

    That all the commanders of departments, after the receipt of this order by them respectively, report severally and directly to the Secretary of War, and that prompt, full, and frequent reports will be expected of all and each of them.

                           Abraham Lincoln

Lincoln's order of March 11, 1862 *(above)* removed General George McClellan *(top, right)* from the post of general-in-chief of all Union armies but left him in charge of the Army of the Potomac. Lincoln hoped the change would free McClellan to concentrate on the Peninsula Campaign, but Confederate forces led, in part, by General Robert E. Lee *(bottom right)* outmaneuvered and eventually defeated "Little Mac." *ALPLM, CHM*

Union army soldiers wore dark blue jackets, known as sack coats, with light blue pants. Both Union and Confederate forces used a mix of old and new weaponry, such as this modern Enfield rifle from England. *CHM*

Shortly after Willie's death, Lincoln experienced a military nightmare known as the Peninsula Campaign. It occurred from March to June 1862 and involved more than 120,000 men and tons of supplies in a massive effort to capture Richmond, Virginia, the Confederate capital. The Army of the Potomac, commanded by General George B. McClellan, prepared for months, but once in the field, they bogged down and suffered a series of demoralizing defeats by a smaller number of Confederate forces led by generals Joseph E. Johnston and Robert E. Lee. McClellan never launched a serious assault on Richmond, and he eventually made a humiliating retreat back to Washington. Union forces suffered more than fifteen thousand casualties, a shocking number at the time, and Lincoln came under intense criticism for poor military leadership. Some critics, most notably Senator Charles Sumner of Massachusetts, urged Lincoln to attack slavery as a means of defeating the Confederacy, but Lincoln refrained.

Lincoln signed this copy of the Emancipation Proclamation for a charity auction benefitting wounded Union army soldiers. Secretary of State William H. Seward and John Nicolay, Lincoln's private secretary, also signed the document. After the war, Mary Lincoln attested that Lincoln used this pen to sign printed copies of the Proclamation including the one shown here. *ALPLM*

Lincoln likewise met political defeat. Early in his presidency, Lincoln tried to convince the border states (slave states that remained in the Union: Delaware, Maryland, Kentucky, Missouri) to adopt his favored plan of gradual, compensated emancipation. He recommended this approach in his annual message to Congress in December 1861 and subsequently drafted a bill for compensated emancipation in Delaware, the state with the fewest number of slaves (about one thousand). The program would establish an apprentice program for young blacks to learn a trade and slowly end slavery over a thirty-year period. Despite the bill's conservative nature, resistance in the Delaware legislature proved so strong that its supporters did not introduce it. On March 6, 1862, Lincoln submitted a proposal to federally fund emancipation in the border states at a price of $400 per slave. Four days later, he personally met with border state congressmen, but they refused his offer.

On July 12, 1862, Lincoln met again with border state representatives to plead his case, but they still refused. Lincoln attended funeral services later that day for Secretary Stanton's infant son. Riding in a carriage with secretaries Seward and Welles, Lincoln confidentially told them that he had nearly concluded that he must free the slaves or lose the war. Nine days later, Lincoln informed his full cabinet that he planned to issue a formal Emancipation Proclamation if Confederate states did not return to the Union by January 1, 1863. All but Seward and Welles were astonished, and Seward cautioned Lincoln to wait until Union forces scored a major victory before issuing the decree or it would appear to be a desperate measure.

Victory came on September 17, 1862, when Union and Confederate forces met at the Battle of Antietam near the village of Sharpsburg, Maryland. Northern troops under McClellan defeated Lee's army, but at a terrible cost. In all, nearly 5,000 soldiers were killed and 18,500 were wounded, making Antietam the single bloodiest day in American history. Five days later, on September 22, Lincoln issued the Preliminary Emancipation Proclamation, declaring freedom for Southern slaves if the South did not cease hostilities by January 1, 1863.

The Proclamation revealed a radical change in Lincoln's thinking. In his first inaugural address, Lincoln told the South that he had no intention of attacking slavery, but now he made its destruction a chief war aim. When the South failed to surrender by New Year's Day, Lincoln issued the final Emancipation Proclamation that declared immediate freedom for slaves in most rebel territory, empowered Union troops to protect black freedom, and called for the enlistment of former slaves into the Union army. Noticeably absent was any mention of gradual, compensated emancipation or colonization.

Lincoln issued the Proclamation as commander-in-chief, using the only authority he had to strike a blow against slavery, an institution legally protected by the Constitution. The Proclamation served several purposes. First, Lincoln thought it would encourage more slaves to flee their plantations, thus weakening the Confederate home front. Enlisting former slaves into the Union army would increase military manpower. It would appease abolitionist sentiment in England and France and discourage either country from entering the war on the Confederate side. And, finally, Lincoln believed the Proclamation would give the war a higher moral purpose of human liberation.

Lincoln considered the Emancipation Proclamation to be his greatest act as president but he did not mention it in the Gettysburg Address. Instead, Lincoln referred to ending slavery in an indirect manner with phrases such as "the unfinished work" and "the great task remaining before us" that reflected his new mindset about how to save the Union. "Increased devotion to that cause" would, in Lincoln's mind, give "this nation, under God . . . a new birth of freedom" (another veiled reference to emancipation), ensuring "that government of the people, by the people, for the people, shall not perish from the earth."

BLACK SOLDIERS

Lincoln once doubted blacks' military capability and feared their presence in the ranks would discourage white recruitment, but he reversed course with the Emancipation Proclamation. In addition to calling for black troops, Lincoln authorized raising the Fifty-Fourth Massachusetts Volunteer Infantry Regiment, the North's first black military unit, endorsed using blacks in combat as well as noncombat roles, and ordered a mass recruitment of former slaves in the Union-occupied Mississippi Valley. As he wrote to General Grant on August 9, 1863, "I believe [the use of black soldiers] is a resource which, if vigorously applied now, will soon close the contest."

Nearly 180,000 African Americans served in the Union army and nearly 40,000 died. Their courage and dedication to the Union cause helped convince Lincoln toward the end of the war that black veterans should be granted equal citizenship rights. A large majority of black Union soldiers were former slaves who fought for their own freedom and the nation's survival even though they were not yet citizens. At first, black soldiers were typically assigned fatigue duty (nonarmed labor) but as the war continued, they assumed combat roles. However, blacks remained under the command of white officers to assuage Northern white fears about arming blacks. Nor did black soldiers receive the same level of pay or advancement opportunities as white soldiers. Late in the war, Lincoln ordered equal treatment for black soldiers, undoubtedly influenced by a discussion with Frederick Douglass at the White House. Black soldiers, however, continued to serve in segregated units until President Harry S Truman ordered the army's integration in 1948.

Engraved on an ivory whale tooth, this scrimshaw portrait of an African American soldier is from the Carolina coast, site of early efforts to enlist former slaves into the Union army. *CHM*

Three stripes on each sleeve indicate this soldier attained the rank of sergeant. African Americans constituted about 10 precent of the Union army by the end of the Civil War and played a critical role in winning the conflict. *CHM*

The Gettysburg Address is an eloquent testimonial of Lincoln's radical transformation. He had previouly vowed to leave Southern slavery alone, and he sincerely believed that slavery, if confined to the South, would gradually die out on its own. He promoted gradual, not immediate, emancipation, a process that would leave the Union of free and slave states, intact and unharmed. But, profoundly transformed by war, Lincoln now believed that ending slavery would save the Union and its founding ideals forever.

Abraham Lincoln, February 5, 1865. Photograph by Alexander Gardner, Washington, D.C. *ALPLM*
Facing page, backdrop: Lincoln letter with passage from the Second Inaugural Address, March 20, 1865 (detail). *ALPLM*

CHAPTER 4
THE SECOND INAUGURAL ADDRESS

"EACH LOOKED FOR AN EASIER TRIUMPH AND A RESULT LESS FUNDAMENTAL AND ASTOUNDING."

Abraham Lincoln delivered his second inaugural address on March 4, 1865. Many people consider it to be Lincoln's greatest speech, even surpassing the Gettysburg Address. It certainly differs from other Lincoln speeches in its religious tone and moral gravity. In the words of Frederick Douglass, the speech was "a sacred effort," not only a rhetorical masterpiece but also a deeply moving revelation of Lincoln's personal transformation.

To set the stage: Lincoln ran for reelection in 1864 against former Union army commander George B. McClellan. McClellan appealed to many Northerners who were tired of war and unsure about Lincoln's emancipation policy. Lincoln's reelection seemed highly unlikely during the summer of 1864 when the war bogged down, causing massive casualties and widespread despair in the North. On September 3, however, Union forces under General William T. Sherman captured Atlanta, a crucial victory that sent Northern spirits soaring and gave Lincoln a solid chance of winning a second term.

Despite the tumult of war, Lincoln insisted on holding the presidential election to uphold the Constitution and reassure Northerners that the institutions of democracy remained in place and viable. Lincoln did not run as a Republican, however, but rather as a candidate of the National Union Party, formed by his supporters in June 1864 to counter the Radical Democracy Party, established by Radical Republicans who felt that Lincoln was not vigorous enough in conducting the war and attacking slavery. They nominated John C. Frémont for president, the first Republican presidential candidate in 1856 and former Union army general reprimanded by Lincoln for declaring freedom for slaves in Missouri in 1861. Frémont eventually dropped out of the race to avoid splitting the Republican vote between himself and Lincoln.

Lincoln and his running mate, Democratic Senator Andrew Johnson of Tennessee, ran against George B. McClellan, the Democratic nominee. His party's platform, fashioned by Peace Democrats, also known as Copperheads, called for a negotiated settlement with the Confederacy that left slavery intact. McClellan agreed with allowing slavery to continue but disagreed with negotiating a peace over achieving a military victory. Nonetheless, he accepted the nomination but placed himself in a contradictory position that diminished his stature with voters. With the capture of Atlanta, the tide turned and swept Lincoln

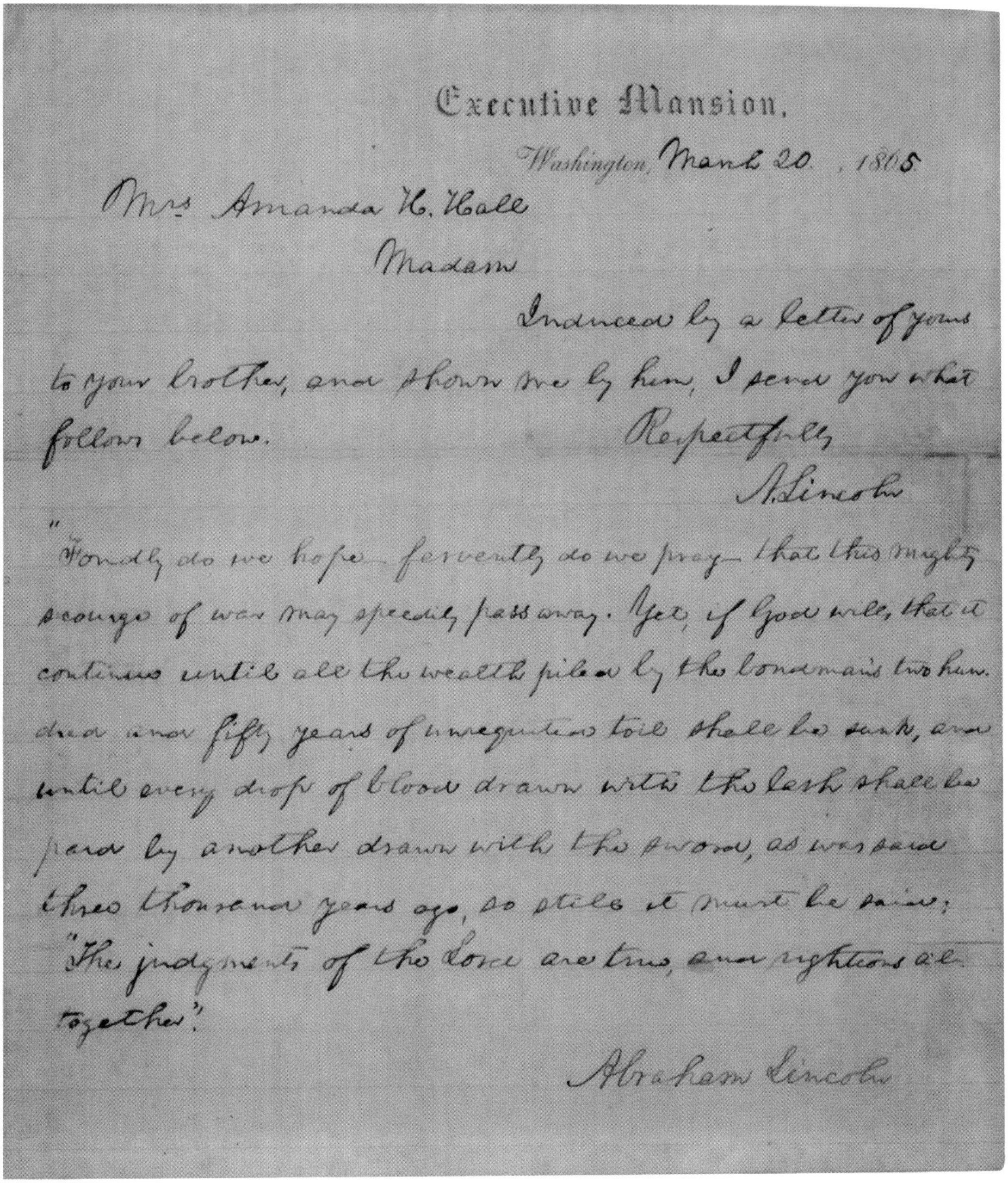

Executive Mansion,

Washington, March 20, 1865

Mrs. Amanda H. Hall

Madam

Induced by a letter of yours to your brother, and shown me by him, I send you what follows below.

Respectfully

A. Lincoln

"Fondly do we hope, fervently do we pray— that this mighty scourge of war may speedily pass away. Yet, if God wills, that it continue until all the wealth piled by the bondsman's two hundred and fifty years of unrequited toil shall be sunk, and until every drop of blood drawn with the lash shall be paid by another drawn with the sword, as was said three thousand years ago, so still it must be said; "The judgments of the Lord are true, and righteous altogether".

Abraham Lincoln

President Lincoln sent this passage of the speech to an admirer, Mrs. Amanda H. Hall, at her request. He described slavery and the Civil War in biblical terms. *ALPLM*

After Atlanta fell to Union forces, noted Civil War photographer George Barnard documented an extensive line of rebel fortifications surrounding the city. Note the heavily damaged home in the distance. *CHM*

to victory. He won all Northern states except Kentucky, New Jersey, and Delaware and captured the Electoral College, 212 to 21. Lincoln also won a large majority of the Union army soldier vote, affirming his role as commander-in-chief.

Four months later, when Lincoln took office for a second time, the North was close to victory. General Sherman's army had occupied a large swath of Confederate territory on its famous March to the Sea, while Lieutenant General Ulysses S. Grant's forces laid siege to Petersburg, gateway to Richmond. The end was near but Lincoln did not celebrate. Instead, he gave one of the greatest speeches in American history. Lincoln first provided a brief update on the military situation, stating that "the progress of our arms, upon which all else depends, is as well known to the public as to myself; and it is, I trust, reasonably satisfactory and encouraging to all." Moving on, Lincoln reflected on the situation four

A colorful glass lantern from the 1864 presidential campaign features Lincoln's portrait and the emblem of the National Union Party, while the ribbon portrays Lincoln and his running mate, Andrew Johnson of Tennessee. *ALPLM*

years earlier, when "all thoughts were anxiously directed to an impending civil-war. . . . Both parties deprecated war; but one would make war rather than let the nation survive; and the other would accept war rather than let it perish. And the war came." But why? For the first time publicly, Lincoln identified slavery as its chief cause, specifically "a peculiar and powerful interest" that wanted to "strengthen, perpetuate, and extend this interest" while the government (his administration) "claimed no right to do more than restrict the territorial enlargement of it."

But, as Lincoln explained, the war wrought unintended consequences. Neither side expected a conflict so massive. Nor did either side anticipate "that the cause of the conflict might cease. . . . Each looked for an easier triumph, and a result less fundamental and astounding." The "astounding" result was, of course, the end of slavery, which Lincoln

Lincoln's efforts to end slavery created controversy, even in the North, as evidenced by this circa 1864 effigy doll that depicts Lincoln as a black man beneath his white face. *ALPL Foundation/Taper Collection*

never intended when he first took office in 1861. The process to end slavery, launched by the Emancipation Proclamation, had been recently furthered by the Thirteenth Amendment, passed by Congress on January 31, 1865.

In the second half of the speech, Lincoln drew powerful lessons for all Americans. Instead of blaming the South, Lincoln pointed out that both sides "read the same Bible, and pray to the same God; and each invokes His aid against the other." He cautioned that when viewing slaveholders, "judge not that we be not judged," reminding Northerners that

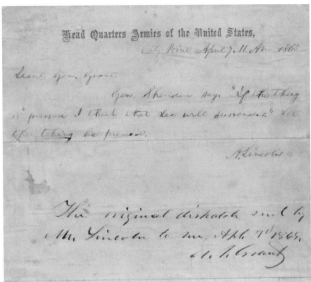

On April 7, 1865, Lincoln sent this telegram message (above) to General Ulysses S. Grant, urging him to end the war. Two days later, Grant (left) accepted Lee's surrender at Appomattox Court House. The writing below Lincoln's is Grant's, authenticating the original dispatch. *CHM*

they, too, had benefitted from the same system that wrung "their bread from the sweat of other men's faces." The "prayers of both," Lincoln continued, "could not be answered; that of neither has been answered fully." Rather, "The Almighty has His own purposes" that allowed slavery to exist and to continue "through His appointed time," but which "He now wills to remove" through "this terrible war." And, if God willed, the war would "continue, until all the wealth piled by the bond-man's two hundred and fifty years of unrequited toil shall be sunk, and until every drop of blood drawn with the lash, shall be paid by another drawn with the sword, as was said three thousand years ago, so still must it be said, 'the judgments of the Lord, are true and righteous altogether.'"

Lincoln implicated all Americans, including himself, in the "offence," or sin, of slavery. He previously accepted Southern slavery in order to maintain the Union. He had not called for abolition but rather endorsed, time after time, a process of gradual, compensated emancipation that would take generations to complete and primarily benefit slaveholders, not slaves, who could return to Africa if they wished. These views had

THE THIRTEENTH AMENDMENT

As president, Lincoln did not have the authority to propose a constitutional amendment abolishing slavery but he came to support the effort to make black freedom permanent. In late 1863, Republican leaders in the Senate introduced the Thirteenth Amendment abolishing slavery throughout the United States. The Senate passed the amendment in April 1864 but the House did not. To ensure its survival, Lincoln had the amendment inserted into his party's political platform and, after his reelection in November, worked with congressional Republicans to ensure its passage in the House on January 31, 1865.

The briefly worded amendment states: "Neither slavery nor involuntary servitude, except as a punishment for crime whereof the party shall have been duly convicted, shall exist within the United States, or any place subject to their jurisdiction." Lincoln declared the amendment "a king's cure for all the evils" and proudly signed his name to several commemorative copies of the document before Secretary of State Seward reminded him that presidents are not supposed to sign constitutional amendments as they do legislative acts.

Congress sent the amendment to state legislatures for ratification, Illinois being the first to do so on February 1, 1865. By December 6, 1865, a required three-fourths of the states—or twenty-seven of thirty-six—had ratified the amendment, including eight former members of the Confederacy: Virginia, Louisiana, Tennessee, Arkansas, South Carolina, Alabama, North Carolina, and Georgia. (Mississippi finally ratified in 1995.) On December 18, 1865, Secretary of State Seward certified that the Thirteenth Amendment had become valid, thus abolishing slavery forever in the United States.

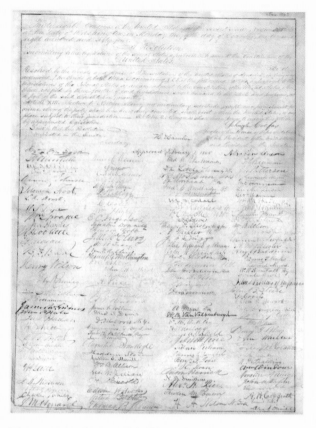

This commemorative copy of the Thirteenth Amendment is signed by President Lincoln, Vice President Hannibal Hamlin, House Speaker Schuyler Colfax, 30 senators, and 108 congressmen. *ALPLM*

Lincoln's Drive through Richmond by Dennis Malone Carter portrays the president's triumphant visit to the fallen rebel capital on April 4, 1865. Throngs of former slaves and white Union sympathizers gave Lincoln a hero's welcome while Confederate supporters remained indoors. CHM

gained Lincoln the presidency, but they also helped perpetuate slavery in defiance of God's will, making the second inaugural address a personal confession of sorts. Lincoln spoke of the slaves' "unrequited toil," implicitly raising the question of whether they deserved compensation for their unpaid labor, and he noted that the terrible violence of the war had been preceded by the terrible violence of slavery. Lincoln closed with a benedictory message of healing and hope for all Americans:

> *With malice toward none; with charity for all; with firmness in the right, as God gives us to see the right, let us strive on to finish the work we are in; to bind up the nation's wounds; to care for him who shall have borne the battle, and for his widow, and his orphan—to do all which may achieve and cherish a just, and a lasting peace, among ourselves, and with all nations.*

Abraham Lincoln, March 6, 1865. Photograph by
Henry Warren, Washington, D.C. *ALPLM*
Facing page, backdrop: Lincoln's Speech on
Reconstruction, 1905 printing (detail). *ALPLM*

By these recent successes the reinauguration
of the national authority—reconstruction—
which has had a large share of thought from the
first, is pressed much more closely upon our attention. It is fraught with great difficulty.
Unlike a case of war between independent nations, there is no authorized organ for us to treat
with—no one man has authority to give up the
rebellion for any other man. We simply must
begin with and mold from disorganized and discordant elements. Nor is it a small addition
embarrassment that we, the loyal people, differ
among ourselves as to the mode, manner, and
measure of reconstruction. As a general rule,
I abstain from reading the reports of attacks
upon myself, wishing not to be provoked by that
to which I cannot properly offer an answer. In
spite of this precaution, however, it comes to my
knowledge that I am much censured for some

CHAPTER 5

THE SPEECH ON
RECONSTRUCTION

"I WOULD MYSELF PREFER THAT IT [THE ELECTIVE FRANCHISE] WERE NOW CONFERRED ON THE VERY INTELLIGENT, AND ON THOSE WHO SERVE OUR CAUSE AS SOLDIERS."

On the evening of April 11, 1865, Lincoln spoke from a window overlooking the south door of the Executive Mansion to a large crowd of people gathered below. They were celebrating the end of the Civil War with Lee's surrender at Appomattox Court House two days before, and the festive mood meant few people paid close attention to the president's speech, which focused on putting the nation back together again. Lincoln's Speech on Reconstruction would be his last public address, and it remains one of his most significant for suggesting a new future for America as a biracial democracy, the first in world history.

Lincoln began, "We meet this evening, not in sorrow, but in gladness of heart. The evacuation of Petersburg and Richmond, and the surrender of the principal insurgent army, give hope of a righteous and speedy peace whose joyous expression cannot be restrained." After acknowledging "He, from Whom all blessings flow" and the army, Lincoln pointed out that "reconstruction . . . is pressed much more closely upon our attention. It is fraught with great difficulty . . . there is no authorized organ for us to treat with. . . . We simply must begin with, and mould from, disorganized and discordant elements."

In actuality, Lincoln had developed a preliminary plan to restore the Union, known as the Proclamation of Amnesty and Reconstruction, submitted to Congress on December 8, 1863. The plan granted a full pardon and return of property, except slaves, to all persons engaged in the rebellion except for the highest Confederate officials and military officers. It also allowed new state governments to be formed when 10 percent of the eligible voters of 1860 (all of them white) had taken an oath of allegiance to the United States. Finally, Southern states readmitted to the Union in this fashion were encouraged to enact plans to deal with freed slaves without compromising their freedom. Lincoln's Ten Percent Plan, as it was known, seized the initiative for Reconstruction from Congress, but its lenient terms angered Radical Republicans led by Thaddeus Stevens of Pennsylvania who wanted to set more stringent terms.

Lincoln focused the next part of his speech on Louisiana, the first state to experience reconstruction. He noted that Louisiana stood ready for readmission to the Union with a new state government and some twelve thousand voters who had

Lincoln died in this bed on the morning of April 15, 1865, after being shot the night before by John Wilkes Booth at Ford's Theatre. Booth, a well-known actor and Confederate sympathizer, had been present at Lincoln's last speech and vowed to kill the president after hearing him suggest giving equal voting rights to some blacks. This view of the bed, taken at the Chicago History Museum, includes *Lincoln's Last Hours*, painted by Alonzo Chappel in 1868. *CHM*

As illustrated by this poster, Booth remained at large for several days after killing Lincoln. The poster also depicts two members of Booth's shadowy conspiracy ring, John Surratt and David Herold. *ALPL Foundation/Taper Collection*

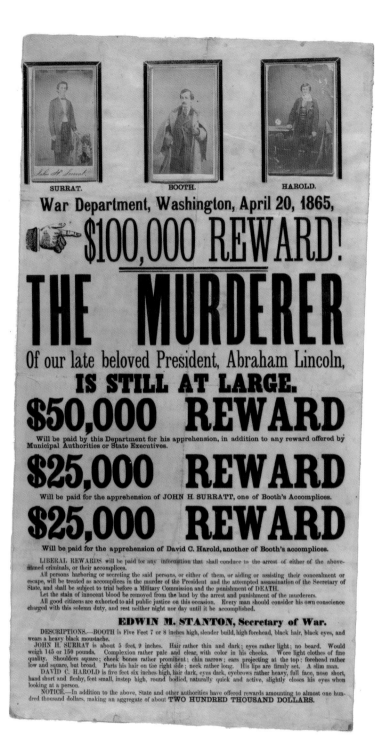

On July 7, 1865, the federal government executed four people for conspiring to assassinate Lincoln: (left to right) Mary Surratt, Lewis Powell, David Herold, and George Atzerodt. Alexander Gardner, assisted by Timothy H. O'Sullivan, captured the grisly scene. *CHM*

sworn allegiance to the Union but that the "amount of constituency . . . would be more satisfactory . . . if it contained fifty, thirty, or even twenty thousand." Lincoln noted that some (especially Louisiana's free black community and Northern abolitionists and Radicals) were displeased that "the elective franchise (the right to vote) is not given to the colored man" and claimed that, "I would myself prefer that it were now conferred on the very intelligent, and on those who serve our cause as soldiers."

Though limited, Lincoln's suggestion is the first time an American president publicly endorsed the extension of equal voting rights to blacks. He himself had long believed that blacks were not entitled to the same voting rights as whites, and his stunning reversal in this speech marks a watershed moment, a turning away from the past toward a future day when people of different races would be part of a "government of the people, by the people, for the people." His thinking had evolved on the issue of racial equality, as it had on black freedom. The service of nearly two hundred thousand black soldiers in the Union war effort, as well as several meetings at the White House with noted African Americans, such as Frederick Douglass, helped to convince Lincoln that black Americans deserved equal citizenship.

Undertaker's assistant Mose Sandford mailed this letter to his "friend Jonny" along with a small bit of Lincoln's shirt. Sandford had been offered large sums for various souvenirs, but he sent this piece only out of friendship. *ALPL Foundation/Taper Collection*

Lincoln continued his speech with a plea to support Louisiana's effort, including "empowering the Legislature to confer the elective franchise upon the colored man." "Now," said Lincoln, "if we reject, and spurn them [Louisiana's new state government], we do our utmost to disorganize and disperse them," and continued:

> We in effect say to the white men, "You are worthless, or worse, we will neither help you, nor be helped by you." To the blacks we say "This cup of liberty which these, your old masters, hold to your lips, we will dash from you, and leave you to the chances of gathering the spilled and scattered contents in some vague and undefined when, where, and how."

If, on the other hand, the North supports their efforts, "We encourage the hearts, and nerve the arms of the twelve thousand to adhere to their work" and inspire blacks, too, "with vigilance, and energy, and daring." Lincoln followed with an analogy: "Concede

Tucked into Lincoln's left-hand coat pocket at the time of the shooting, these gloves were kept for a time by Mary Lincoln, then given or sold to presidential memorabilia collector Benjamin Richardson.
ALPL Foundation/Taper Collection

Soldiers guarding Ford's Theatre after the shooting also collected souvenirs. Sgt. George Sizer, an immigrant, sent items to his fiancée back in Iowa, including bits of fabric from the presidential box.
Courtesy of a Private Collection

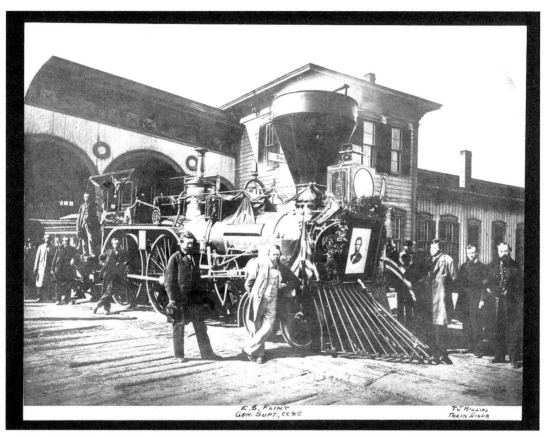

Despite traveling sixteen hundred miles from east to west, Lincoln's funeral train was rarely photographed so well as in Cleveland on April 28, 1865. The Lincoln portrait over the cowcatcher had to be changed periodically. *ALPL Foundation / Taper Collection*

that the new government of Louisiana is only to what it should be as the egg is to the fowl, we shall sooner have the fowl by hatching the egg than by smashing it?" As a final point, Lincoln argued that if "we reject Louisiana, we also reject one vote in favor of the proposed amendment to the national constitution," a reference to the Thirteenth Amendment abolishing slavery. The Louisiana legislature had ratified the amendment several weeks earlier, on February 17, 1865, becoming the seventeenth state to approve the measure. Some critics believed that only Northern states had to be involved in the process, but Lincoln stated in this speech that "such a ratification would be questionable" while having three-fourths of *all* the States, as required by the Constitution, "would be unquestioned and unquestionable." Lincoln would have his way, with nineteen Northern and eight Southern states ratifying the amendment by December 6, 1865 to make it part of the Constitution.

The War Department printed exact itineraries for each leg of the funeral train's journey. Between Cleveland and Columbus, Ohio, the train passed through twenty-two towns. *ALPL Foundation/ Taper Collection*

Cleveland, Columbus & Cincinnati R. R.

SPECIAL TIME SCHEDULE

FOR THE TRAIN CONVEYING THE

REMAINS OF ABRAHAM LINCOLN, LATE PRESIDENT OF THE U.S., AND ESCORT,

FROM WASHINGTON, D. C., TO SPRINGFIELD, ILL.

Cleveland to Columbus, Saturday, April 29th, 1865.

Leave Cleveland	12.00	Midnight.
Berea	12.43	A. M.
Olmsted	12.51	"
Columbia	1.02	"
Grafton	1.23	"
La Grange	1.37	"
Wellington	2.00	"
Rochester	2.17	"
New London	2.36	"
Greenwich	2.59	"
Shiloh	3.19	"
Shelby	3.39	"
Crestline	4.07	"
Galion	4.23	"
Iberia	4.41	"
Gilead	5.05	"
Cardington	5.20	"
Ashley	5.43	"
Eden	5.55	"
Berlin	6.19	"
Lewis Centre	6.32	"
Orange	6.37	"
Worthington	6.56	"
Arrive Columbus	7.30	A. M.

This Train will have exclusive right to the Road against all other Trains. A Pilot Locomotive will be run ten minutes in advance of the above Schedule time.

E. S. FLINT, Superintendent.

SANFORD & HAYWARD, PRINTERS, CLEVELAND.

On May 4, 1865, Lincoln's remains and those of his son Willie were placed in a temporary receiving vault at Oak Ridge Cemetery in Springfield, Illinois. Ridgway Glover of Philadelphia captured the somber scene. *ALPLM*

Lincoln followed with a rhetorical question, "Can Louisiana be brought into proper practical relations with the Union *sooner* by sustaining or by *discarding* her new State Government?" Lincoln answered, "What has been said of Louisiana will apply generally to other States" and, yet, so many "great peculiarities" pertain to each state "that no exclusive, and inflexible plan can safely by prescribed" to the entire South. It "would surely become a new entanglement," but important principles, implying the end of slavery,

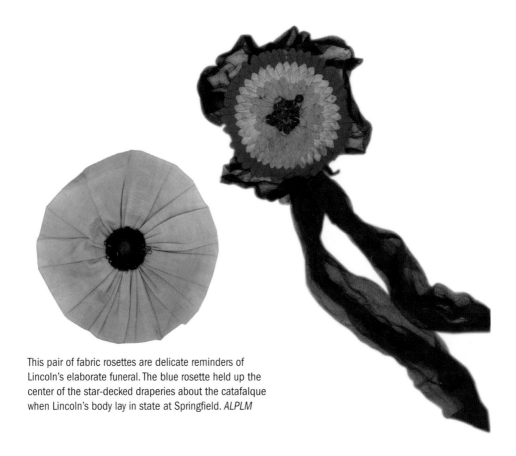

This pair of fabric rosettes are delicate reminders of Lincoln's elaborate funeral. The blue rosette held up the center of the star-decked draperies about the catafalque when Lincoln's body lay in state at Springfield. *ALPLM*

"may, and must, be inflexible." In conclusion, Lincoln said that it may be his duty to make a new announcement regarding Reconstruction "to the people of the South" and that he would not fail to act "when satisfied that action will be proper."

Lincoln knew that great challenges lay ahead. The Civil War had resolved two fundamental issues—slavery and secession—but a host of troubling questions remained, the most crucial being about the Southern states' restored relationship to the federal government and the freedman's new role in American society. Lincoln had a basic plan of restoring the Union, and he endorsed equal citizenship for some blacks, but what would he do next? Unfortunately, the question can't be answered. John Wilkes Booth, a well-known actor and Confederate sympathizer, attended Lincoln's Reconstruction speech, and, when he heard Lincoln suggest black voting rights, he reportedly said, "That means nigger citizenship. Now, by God, I'll put him through." Three days later, on the evening of April 14, 1865, Booth shot Lincoln at Ford's Theatre. Carried across the street to the Petersen House, the mortally wounded president died early the next morning, plunging the war-torn nation into an even deeper grief and leaving many issues unresolved.

EPILOGUE: FROM FREEDOM TO EQUALITY

Lincoln brought the nation closer to its founding ideals of human freedom and equality but the road proved long and difficult. The process began in the Civil War with the Emancipation Proclamation and Thirteenth Amendment, but citizenship rights for former slaves remained uncertain. In 1866, Congress, after a bitter debate, passed the Fourteenth Amendment, making all persons born or naturalized in the United States full citizens, including former slaves. Although state ratification proved equally contentious, the amendment finally became law in July 1868.

The next steps proved even more arduous. Reconstruction Acts passed in 1867 called for black suffrage in the South but not in the North, where half of the states did not allow blacks to vote in elections. Radical Republicans pushed for a constitutional amendment guaranteeing black suffrage in all states and, after much wrangling, drafted an amendment that passed Congress on February 26, 1869. The briefly worded document read: "The right of citizens of the United States to vote shall not be denied or abridged by the United States or by any state on account of race, color, or previous condition of servitude." It became part of the Constitution on March 30, 1870. The South, however, continued to resist with acts of violence by white supremacist groups such as the Ku Klux Klan and, after the end of Reconstruction, by imposing severe restrictions on black voters that remained in place until the Voting Rights Act of 1965 made these actions illegal.

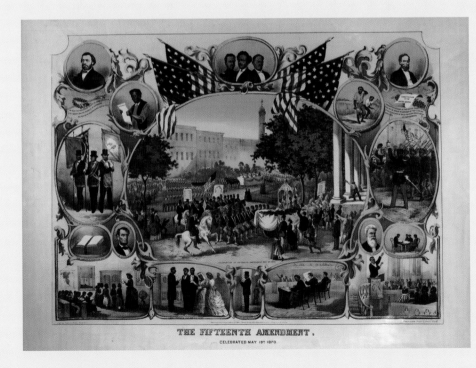

THE FIFTEENTH AMENDMENT.
CELEBRATED MAY 19th 1870.

A colorful print celebrating the Fifteenth Amendment is replete with images of black heroes and achievement. Also present on the lower left side is a portrait of Abraham Lincoln, the first president to propose equal voting rights for African Americans. *ALPLM*

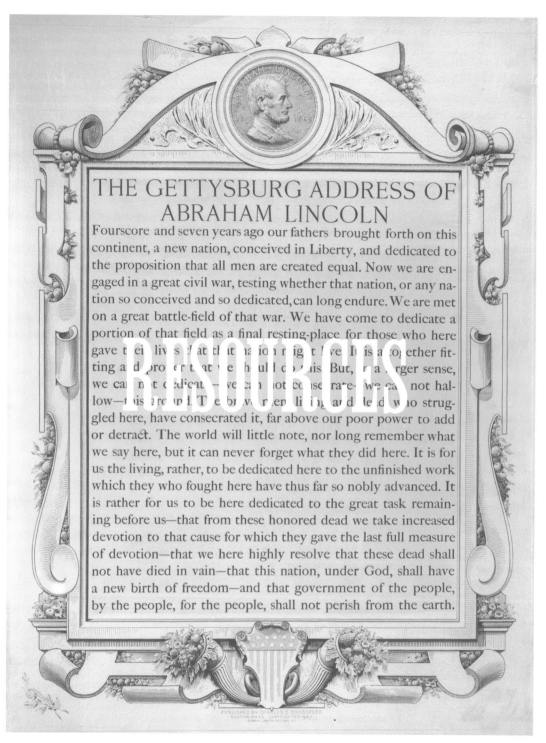

THE GETTYSBURG ADDRESS OF ABRAHAM LINCOLN

Fourscore and seven years ago our fathers brought forth on this continent, a new nation, conceived in Liberty, and dedicated to the proposition that all men are created equal. Now we are engaged in a great civil war, testing whether that nation, or any nation so conceived and so dedicated, can long endure. We are met on a great battle-field of that war. We have come to dedicate a portion of that field as a final resting-place for those who here gave their lives that that nation might live. It is altogether fitting and proper that we should do this. But, in a larger sense, we can not dedicate—we can not consecrate—we can not hallow—this ground. The brave men, living and dead, who struggled here, have consecrated it, far above our poor power to add or detract. The world will little note, nor long remember what we say here, but it can never forget what they did here. It is for us the living, rather, to be dedicated here to the unfinished work which they who fought here have thus far so nobly advanced. It is rather for us to be here dedicated to the great task remaining before us—that from these honored dead we take increased devotion to that cause for which they gave the last full measure of devotion—that we here highly resolve that these dead shall not have died in vain—that this nation, under God, shall have a new birth of freedom—and that government of the people, by the people, for the people, shall not perish from the earth.

PUBLISHED BY CHARLES E. GOODSPEED
BOSTON, MASS. COPYRIGHTED 1907
SIDNEY L. SMITH DEL AND SC.

Tribute to Abraham Lincoln and the Gettysburg Address. Ornamented by Sidney L. Smith, published in Boston, 1907. *ALPLM*

A HOUSE DIVIDED

Delivered June 16, 1858, Springfield, Illinois

Mr. PRESIDENT and Gentlemen of the Convention.

If we could first know *where* we are, and *whither* we are tending, we could then better judge *what* to do, and *how* to do it.

We are now far into the *fifth* year, since a policy was initiated, with the *avowed* object, and *confident* promise, of putting an end to slavery agitation.

Under the operation of that policy, that agitation has not only, *not ceased*, but has *constantly augmented*.

In my opinion, it *will* not cease, until a *crisis* shall have been reached, and passed.

"A house divided against itself cannot stand."

I believe this government cannot endure, permanently half *slave* and half *free*.

I do not expect the Union to be *dissolved*—I do not expect the house to *fall*—but I *do* expect it will cease to be divided.

It will become *all* one thing, or *all* the other.

Either the *opponents* of slavery, will arrest the further spread of it, and place it where the public mind shall rest in the belief that it is in course of ultimate extinction; or its *advocates* will push it forward, till it shall become alike lawful in *all* the States, *old* as well as *new*— *North* as well as *South*.

Have we no *tendency* to the latter condition?

Let any one who doubts, carefully contemplate that now almost complete legal combination—piece of *machinery* so to speak—compounded of the Nebraska doctrine, and the Dred Scott decision. Let him consider not only *what work* the machinery is adapted to do, and how well adapted; but also, let him study the *history* of its construction, and trace, if he can, or rather *fail*, if he can, to trace the evidences of design, and concert of action, among its chief bosses, from the beginning.

But, so far, *Congress* only, had acted; and an indorsement by the people, *real* or apparent, was indispensable, to *save* the point already gained, and give chance for more.

The new year of 1854 found slavery excluded from more than half the States by State Constitutions, and from most of the national territory by Congressional prohibition.

Four days later, commenced the struggle, which ended in repealing that Congressional prohibition.

This opened all the national territory to slavery; and was the first point gained.

This necessity had not been overlooked; but had been provided for, as well as might be, in the notable argument of "*squatter sovereignty*," otherwise called "*sacred right of self government*," which latter phrase, though expressive of the only rightful basis of any government, was so perverted in this attempted use of it as to amount to just this: That if any *one* man, choose to enslave *another*, no *third* man shall be allowed to object.

That argument was incorporated into the Nebraska bill itself, in the language which follows: "It being the true intent and meaning of this act not to legislate slavery into any Territory or state, nor to exclude it therefrom; but to leave the people thereof perfectly free to form and regulate their domestic institutions in their own way, subject only to the Constitution of the United States."

Then opened the roar of loose declamation in favor of "Squatter Sovereignty," and "Sacred right of self government."

"But," said opposition members, "let us be more *specific*—let us *amend* the bill so as to expressly declare that the people of the territory *may* exclude slavery." "Not we," said the friends of the measure; and down they voted the amendment.

While the Nebraska bill was passing through congress, a *law case*, involving the question of a negroe's freedom, by reason of his owner having voluntarily taken him first into a free state and then a territory covered by the congressional prohibition, and held him as a slave, for a long time in each, was passing through the U.S. Circuit Court for the District of Missouri; and both Nebraska bill and law suit were brought to a decision in the same month of May, 1854. The negroe's name was "Dred Scott," which name now designates the decision finally made in the case.

Before the *then* next Presidential election, the law case came *to*, and was argued *in* the Supreme Court of the United States; but the *decision* of it was deferred until *after* the election. Still, *before* the election, Senator

Trumbull, on the floor of the Senate, requests the leading advocate of the Nebraska bill to state *his opinion* whether the people of a territory can constitutionally exclude slavery from their limits; and the latter answers, "That is a question for the Supreme Court."

The election came. Mr. Buchanan was elected, and the *indorsement*, such as it was, secured. That was the *second* point gained. The indorsement, however, fell short of a clear popular majority by nearly four hundred thousand votes, and so, perhaps, was not overwhelmingly reliable and satisfactory.

The *outgoing* President, in his last annual message, as impressively as possible *echoed back* upon the people the *weight* and *authority* of the indorsement.

The Supreme Court met again; *did not* announce their decision, but ordered a re-argument.

The Presidential inauguration came, and still no decision of the court; but the *incoming* President, in his inaugural address, fervently exhorted the people to abide by the forthcoming decision, *whatever it might be.*

Then, in a few days, came the decision.

The reputed author of the Nebraska bill finds an early occasion to make a speech at this capitol indorsing the Dred Scott Decision, and vehemently denouncing all opposition to it.

The new President, too, seizes the early occasion of the Silliman letter to *indorse* and strongly *construe* that decision, and to express his *astonishment* that any different view had ever been entertained.

At length a squabble springs up between the President and the author of the Nebraska bill, on the *mere* question of *fact*, whether the Lecompton constitution was or was not, in any just sense, made by the people of Kansas; and in that squabble the latter declares that all he wants is a fair vote for the people, and that he *cares* not whether slavery be voted *down* or voted *up.* I do not understand his declaration that he cares not whether slavery be voted down or voted up, to be intended by him other than as an *apt definition* of the *policy* he would impress upon the public mind—the *principle* for which he declares he has suffered much, and is ready to suffer to the end.

And well may he cling to that principle. If he has any parental feeling, well may he cling to it. That principle, is the only *shred* left of his original Nebraska doctrine. Under the Dred Scott decision, "squatter sovereignty" squatted out of existence, tumbled down like temporary scaffolding—like the mould at the foundry served through

one blast and fell back into loose sand—helped to carry an election, and then was kicked to the winds. His late *joint* struggle with the Republicans, against the Lecompton Constitution, involves nothing of the original Nebraska doctrine. That struggle was made on a point, the right of a people to make their own constitution, upon which he and the Republicans have never differed.

The several points of the Dred Scott decision, in connection with Senator Douglas' "care not" policy, constitute the piece of machinery, in its *present* state of advancement. This was the third point gained.

The *working* points of that machinery are:

First, that no negro slave, imported as such from Africa, and no descendant of such slave can ever be a *citizen* of any State, in the sense of that term as used in the Constitution of the United States.

This point is made in order to deprive the negro, in every possible event, of the benefit of this provision of the United States Constitution, which declares that—

"The citizens of each State shall be entitled to all privileges and immunities of citizens in the several States."

Secondly, that "subject to the Constitution of the United States," neither *Congress* nor a *Territorial Legislature* can exclude slavery from any United States territory.

This point is made in order that individual men may *fill up* the territories with slaves, without danger of losing them as property, and thus to enhance the chances of *permanency* to the institution through all the future.

Thirdly, that whether the holding a negro in actual slavery in a free State, makes him free, as against the holder, the United States courts will not decide, but will leave to be decided by the courts of any slave State the negro may be forced into by the master.

This point is made, not to be pressed *immediately*; but, if acquiesced in for a while, and apparently *indorsed* by the people at an election, *then* to sustain the logical conclusion that what Dred Scott's master might lawfully do with Dred Scott, in the free State of Illinois, every other master may lawfully do with any other *one*, or one *thousand* slaves, in Illinois, or in any other free State.

Auxiliary to all this, and working hand in hand with it, the Nebraska doctrine, or what is left of it, is to *educate* and *mould* public opinion, at least *Northern* public opinion, to not *care* whether slavery is voted *down* or voted *up.*

This shows exactly where we now *are*; and *partially* also, whither we are tending.

It will throw additional light on the latter, to go back, and run the mind over the string of historical facts already stated. Several things will *now* appear less *dark* and *mysterious* than they did when they were transpiring. The people were to be left "perfectly free" "subject only to the Constitution." What the *Constitution* had to do with it, outsiders could not *then* see. Plainly enough *now*, it was an exactly fitted *niche*, for the Dred Scott decision to afterwards come in, and declare the *perfect freedom* of the people, to be just no freedom at all.

Why was the amendment, expressly declaring the right of the people to exclude slavery, voted down? Plainly enough *now*, the adoption of it, would have spoiled the niche for the Dred Scott decision.

Why was the court decision held up? Why, even a Senator's individual opinion withheld, till *after* the Presidential election? Plainly enough *now*, the speaking out *then* would have damaged the "*perfectly free*" argument upon which the election was to be carried.

Why the *outgoing* President's felicitation on the indorsement? Why the delay of a reargument? Why the incoming President's *advance* exhortation in favor of the decision?

These things *look* like the cautious *patting* and petting a spirited horse, preparatory to mounting him, when it is dreaded that he may give the rider a fall.

And why the hasty after indorsements of the decision by the President and others?

We can not absolutely *know* that all these exact adaptations are the result of preconcert. But when we see a lot of framed timbers, different portions of which we know have been gotten out at different times and places and by different workmen—Stephen, Franklin, Roger and James, for instance—and when we see these timbers joined together, and see they exactly make the frame of a house or a mill, all the tenons and mortices exactly fitting, and all the lengths and proportions of the different pieces exactly adapted to their respective places, and not a piece too many or too few—not omitting even scaffolding—or, if a single piece be lacking, we can see the place in the frame exactly fitted and prepared to yet bring such piece in—in *such* a case, we find it impossible to not *believe* that Stephen and Franklin and Roger and James all understood one another from the beginning, and all worked upon a common *plan* or *draft* drawn up before the first lick was struck.

It should not be overlooked that, by the Nebraska bill, the people of a *State* as well as *Territory*, were to be left "*perfectly free*" "*subject only to the Constitution.*"

Why mention a *State*? They were legislating for *territories*, and not *for* or *about* States. Certainly the people of a State *are* and *ought to be* subject to the Constitution of the United States; but why is mention of this *lugged* into this merely *territorial* law? Why are the people of a *territory* and the people of a state therein *lumped* together, and their relation to the Constitution therein treated as being *precisely* the same?

While the opinion of *the Court*, by Chief Justice Taney, in the Dred Scott case, and the separate opinions of all the concurring Judges, expressly declare that the Constitution of the United States neither permits Congress nor a Territorial legislature to exclude slavery from any United States territory, they all *omit* to declare whether or not the same Constitution permits a *state*, or the people of a State, to exclude it.

Possibly, this was a mere *omission*; but who can be *quite* sure, if McLean or Curtis had sought to get into the opinion a declaration of unlimited power in the people of a state to exclude slavery from their limits, just as Chase and Macy sought to get such declaration, in behalf of the people of a *territory*, into the Nebraska bill—I ask, who can be quite *sure* that it would not have been voted down, in the one case, as it had been in the other.

The nearest approach to the point of declaring the power of a State over slavery, is made by Judge Nelson. He approaches it more than once, using the precise idea, and *almost* the language too, of the Nebraska act. On one occasion his exact language is, "except in cases where the power is restrained by the Constitution of the United States, the law of the State is supreme over the subject of slavery within its jurisdiction."

In what *cases* the power of the *states is* so restrained by the U.S. Constitution, is left an open question, precisely as the same question, as to the restraint on the power of the *territories* was left open in the Nebraska act. Put that and that together, and we have another nice little niche, which we may, ere long, see filled with another Supreme Court decision, declaring that the Constitution of the United States does not permit a *state* to exclude slavery from its limits.

And this may especially be expected if the doctrine of "care not whether slavery be voted *down* or voted *up*," shall gain upon the public mind sufficiently to give promise that such a decision can be maintained when made.

Such a decision is all that slavery now lacks of being alike lawful in all the States.

Welcome or unwelcome, such decision *is* probably coming, and will soon be upon us, unless the power of the present political dynasty shall be met and overthrown.

We shall *lie down* pleasantly dreaming that the people of *Missouri* are on the verge of making their State *free*; and we shall *awake* to the reality, instead, that the *Supreme* Court has made *Illinois* a *slave* State.

To meet and overthrow the power of that dynasty, is the work now before all those who would prevent that consummation.

That is *what* we have to do.

But *how* can we best do it?

There are those who denounce us *openly* to their *own* friends, and yet whisper *us softly*, that *Senator Douglas* is the *aptest* instrument there is, with which to effect that object. *They* do *not* tell us, nor has *he* told us, that he *wishes* any such object to be effected. They wish us to *infer* all, from the facts, that he now has a little quarrel with the present head of the dynasty; and that he has regularly voted with us, on a single point, upon which, he and we, have never differed.

They remind us that *he* is a very *great man*, and that the largest of *us* are very small ones. Let this be granted. But "a *living dog* is better than a *dead lion.*" Judge Douglas, if not a *dead* lion *for this work*, is at least a *caged* and *toothless* one. How can he oppose the advances of slavery? He don't *care* anything about it. His avowed *mission is impressing* the "public heart" to *care* nothing about it.

A leading Douglas Democratic newspaper thinks Douglas' superior talent will be needed to resist the revival of the African slave trade.

Does Douglas believe an effort to revive that trade is approaching? He has not said so. Does he *really* think so? But if it is, how can he resist it? For years he has labored to prove it a *sacred right* of white men to take negro slaves into the new territories. Can he possibly show that it is less a sacred right to buy them where they can be bought cheapest? And, unquestionably they can be bought *cheaper in Africa* than in *Virginia*.

He has done all in his power to reduce the whole question of slavery to one of a mere *right of property*; and as such, how can *he* oppose the foreign slave trade— how can he refuse that trade in that "property" shall be "perfectly free"—unless he does it as a *protection* to the home production? And as the home *producers* will

probably not *ask* the protection, he will be wholly without a ground of opposition.

Senator Douglas holds, we know, that a man may rightfully be *wiser to-day* than he was *yesterday*—that he may rightfully *change* when he finds himself wrong.

But, can we for that reason, run ahead, and *infer* that he *will* make any particular change, of which he, himself, has given no intimation? Can we *safely* base *our* action upon any such vague inference?

Now, as ever, I wish to not *misrepresent* Judge Douglas' *position*, question his *motives*, or do ought that can be personally offensive to him.

Whenever, *if ever*, he and we can come together on *principle* so that *our great cause* may have assistance from *his great ability*, I hope to have interposed no adventitious obstacle.

But clearly, he is not *now* with us—he does not *pretend* to be—he does not *promise* to *ever* be.

Our cause, then, must be intrusted to, and conducted by its own undoubted friends—those whose hands are free, whose hearts are in the work—who do care for the result.

Two years ago the Republicans of the nation mustered over thirteen hundred thousand strong.

We did this under the single impulse of resistance to a common danger, with every external circumstance against us.

Of *strange*, *discordant*, and even, *hostile* elements, we gathered from the four winds, and *formed* and fought the battle through, under the constant hot fire of a disciplined, proud, and pampered enemy.

Did we brave all *then*, to *falter* now?—*now*—when that same enemy is *wavering*, dissevered and belligerent?

The result is not doubtful. We shall not fail—if we stand firm, we shall not fail.

Wise councils may *accelerate* or *mistakes* delay it, but, sooner or later the victory is *sure* to come.

Illinois statehouse, ca. 1858, where Abraham Lincoln delivered the "House Divided" speech. *ALPLM*

FIRST INAUGURAL ADDRESS

Delivered March 4, 1861, U.S. Capitol, Washington, D.C.

Fellow citizens of the United States:

In compliance with a custom as old as the government itself, I appear before you to address you briefly, and to take, in your presence, the oath prescribed by the Constitution of the United States, to be taken by the President "before he enters on the execution of his office."

I do not consider it necessary, at present, for me to discuss those matters of administration about which there is no special anxiety, or excitement.

Apprehension seems to exist among the people of the Southern States, that by the accession of a Republican Administration, their property, and their peace, and personal security, are to be endangered. There has never been any reasonable cause for such apprehension. Indeed, the most ample evidence to the contrary has all the while existed, and been open to their inspection. It is found in nearly all the published speeches of him who now addresses you. I do but quote from one of those speeches when I declare that "I have no purpose, directly or indirectly, to interfere with the institution of slavery in the States where it exists. I believe I have no lawful right to do so, and I have no inclination to do so." Those who nominated and elected me did so with full knowledge that I had made this, and many similar declarations, and had never recanted them. And more than this, they placed in the platform, for my acceptance, and as a law to themselves, and to me, the clear and emphatic resolution which I now read:

"*Resolved*, That the maintenance inviolate of the rights of the States, and especially the right of each State to order and control its own domestic institutions according to its own judgment exclusively, is essential to that balance of power on which the perfection and endurance of our political fabric depend; and we denounce the lawless invasion by armed force of the soil of any State or Territory, no matter under what pretext, as among the gravest of crimes."

I now reiterate these sentiments: and in doing so, I only press upon the public attention the most conclusive evidence of which the case is susceptible, that the property, peace and security of no section are to be in anywise endangered by the now incoming Administration. I add too, that all the protection which, consistently with the Constitution and the laws, can be given, will be cheerfully given to all the States when lawfully demanded, for whatever cause—as cheerfully to one section, now as to another.

There is much controversy about the delivering up of fugitives from service or labor. The clause I now read is as plainly written in the Constitution as any other of its provisions:

"No person held to service or labor in one State, under the laws thereof, escaping into another, shall, in consequence of any law or regulation therein, be discharged from such service or labor, but shall be delivered up on claim of the party to whom such service or labor may be due."

It is scarcely questioned that this provision was intended by those who made it, for the reclaiming of what we call fugitive slaves; and the intention of the law-giver is the law. All members of Congress swear their support to the whole Constitution—to this provision as much as to any other. To the proposition, then, that slaves whose cases come within the terms of this clause, "shall be delivered up," their oaths are unanimous. Now, if they would make the effort in good temper, could they not, with nearly equal unanimity, frame and pass a law, by means of which to keep good that unanimous oath?

There is some difference of opinion whether this clause should be enforced by national or by state authority; but surely that difference is not a very material one. If the slave is to be surrendered, it can be of but little consequence to him, or to others, by which authority it is done. And should any one, in any case, be content that his oath shall go unkept, on a merely unsubstantial controversy as to *how* it shall be kept?

Again, in any law upon this subject, ought not all the safeguards of liberty known in civilized and humane jurisprudence to be introduced, so that a free man be not, in any case, surrendered as a slave? And might it not be well, at the same time, to provide by law for the enforcement of that clause in the Constitution which guarranties that "The citizens of each State shall be entitled to all previleges and immunities of citizens in the several States?"

I take the official oath to-day, with no mental reservations, and with no purpose to construe the Constitution or laws, by any hypercritical rules. And while I do not choose now to specify particular acts of Congress as proper to be enforced, I do suggest, that it will be much safer for all, both in official and private stations, to conform to, and abide by, all those acts which stand unrepealed, than to violate any of them, trusting to find impunity in having them held to be unconstitutional.

It is seventy-two years since the first inauguration of a President under our national Constitution. During that period fifteen different and greatly distinguished citizens, have, in succession, administered the executive branch of the government. They have conducted it through many perils; and, generally, with great success. Yet, with all this scope for precedent, I now enter upon the same task for the brief constitutional term of four years, under great and peculiar difficulty. A disruption of the Federal Union heretofore only menaced, is now formidably attempted.

I hold, that in contemplation of universal law, and of the Constitution, the Union of these States is perpetual. Perpetuity is implied, if not expressed, in the fundamental law of all national governments. It is safe to assert that no government proper, ever had a provision in its organic law for its own termination. Continue to execute all the express provisions of our national Constitution, and the Union will endure forever—it being impossible to destroy it, except by some action not provided for in the instrument itself.

Again, if the United States be not a government proper, but an association of States in the nature of contract merely, can it, as a contract, be peaceably unmade, by less than all the parties who made it? One party to a contract may violate it—break it, so to speak; but does it not require all to lawfully rescind it?

Descending from these general principles, we find the proposition that, in legal contemplation, the Union is perpetual, confirmed by the history of the Union itself. The Union is much older than the Constitution. It was formed in fact, by the Articles of Association in 1774. It was matured and continued by the Declaration of Independence in 1776. It was further matured and the faith of all the then thirteen States expressly plighted and engaged that it should be perpetual, by the Articles of Confederation in 1778. And finally, in 1787, one of the declared objects for ordaining and establishing the Constitution, was "*to form a more perfect union.*"

But if destruction of the Union, by one, or by a part only, of the States, be lawfully possible, the Union is less perfect than before the Constitution, having lost the vital element of perpetuity.

It follows from these views that no State, upon its own mere motion, can lawfully get out of the Union,—that *resolves* and *ordinances* to that effect are legally void; and that acts of violence, within any State or States, against the authority of the United States, are insurrectionary or revolutionary, according to circumstances.

I therefore consider that, in view of the Constitution and the laws, the Union is unbroken; and, to the extent of my ability, I shall take care, as the Constitution itself expressly enjoins upon me, that the laws of the Union be faithfully executed in all the States. Doing this I deem to be only a simple duty on my part; and I shall perform it, so far as practicable, unless my rightful masters, the American people, shall withhold the requisite means, or, in some authoritative manner, direct the contrary. I trust this will not be regarded as a menace, but only as the declared purpose of the Union that it *will* constitutionally defend, and maintain itself.

In doing this there needs to be no bloodshed or violence; and there shall be none, unless it be forced upon the national authority. The power the confided to me, will be used to hold, occupy, and possess the property, and places belonging to the government, and to collect the duties and imposts; but beyond what may be necessary for these objects, there will be no invasion—no using of force against, or among the people anywhere. Where hostility to the United States, in any interior locality, shall be so great and so universal, as to prevent competent resident citizens from holding the Federal offices, there will be no attempt to force obnoxious strangers among the people for that object. While the strict legal right may exist in the government to enforce the exercise of these offices, the attempt to do so would be so irritating, and so nearly impracticable with all, that I deem it better to forego, for the time, the uses of such offices.

The mails, unless repelled, will continue to be furnished in all parts of the Union. So far as possible, the people everywhere shall have that sense of perfect security which is most favorable to calm thought and reflection. The course here indicated will be followed, unless current events, and experience, shall show a modification, or change, to be proper; and in every case and exigency, my best discretion will be exercised, according to circumstances actually existing, and with a view and a hope of a peaceful solution of the national troubles, and the restoration of fraternal sympathies and affections.

That there are persons in one section, or another who seek to destroy the Union at all events, and are glad of any pretext to do it, I will neither affirm or deny; but if there be such, I need address no word to them. To those, however, who really love the Union, may I not speak?

Before entering upon so grave a matter as the destruction of our national fabric, with all its benefits, its memories, and its hopes, would it not be wise to ascertain precisely why we do it? Will you hazard so desperate a step, while there is any possibility that any portion of the ills you fly from, have no real existence? Will you, while the certain ills you fly to, are greater than all the real ones you fly from? Will you risk the commission of so fearful a mistake?

All profess to be content in the Union, if all constitutional rights can be maintained. Is it true, then, that any right, plainly written in the Constitution, has been denied? I think not. Happily the human mind is so constituted, that no party can reach to the audacity of doing this. Think, if you can, of a single instance in which a plainly written provision of the Constitution has ever been denied. If, by the mere force of numbers, a majority should deprive a minority of any clearly written constitutional right, it might, in a moral point of view, justify revolution—certainly would, if such right were a vital one. But such is not our case. All the vital rights of minorities, and of individuals, are so plainly assured to them, by affirmations and negations, guarranties and prohibitions, in the Constitution, that controversies never arise concerning them. But no organic law can ever be framed with a provision specifically applicable to every question which may occur in practical administration. No foresight can anticipate, nor any document of reasonable length contain express provisions for all possible questions. Shall fugitives from labor be surrendered by national or by State authority? The Constitution does not expressly say. *May* Congress prohibit slavery in the territories? The Constitution does not expressly say. *Must* Congress protect slavery in the territories? The Constitution does not expressly say.

From questions of this class spring all our constitutional controversies, and we divide upon them into majorities and minorities. If the minority will not acquiesce, the majority must, or the government must cease. There is no other alternative; for continuing the government, is acquiescence on one side or the other. If a minority, in such case, will secede rather than acquiesce, they make a precedent which, in turn, will divide and ruin them; for a minority of their own will secede from them, whenever a majority refuses to be controlled by such minority. For instance, why may not any portion of a new confederacy, a year or two hence, arbitrarily secede again, precisely as portions of the present Union now claim to secede from it. All who cherish disunion sentiments, are now being educated to the exact temper of doing this. Is there such perfect identity of interests among the States to compose a new Union, as to produce harmony only, and prevent renewed secession?

Plainly, the central idea of secession, is the essence of anarchy. A majority, held in restraint by constitutional checks, and limitations, and always changing easily, with deliberate changes of popular opinions and sentiments, is the only true sovereign of a free people. Whoever rejects it, does, of necessity, fly to anarchy or to despotism. Unanimity is impossible; the rule of a minority, as a permanent arrangement, is wholly inadmissable; so that, rejecting the majority principle, anarchy, or despotism in some form, is all that is left.

I do not forget the position assumed by some, that constitutional questions are to be decided by the Supreme Court; nor do I deny that such decisions must be binding in any case, upon the parties to a suit, as to the object of that suit, while they are also entitled to very high respect and consideration, in all paralel cases, by all other departments of the government. And while it is obviously possible that such decision may be erroneous in any given case, still the evil effect following it, being limited to that particular case, with the chance that it may be over-ruled, and never become a precedent for other cases, can better be borne than could the evils of a different practice. At the same time the candid citizen must confess that if the policy of the government, upon vital questions, affecting the whole people, is to be irrevocably fixed by decisions of the Supreme Court, the instant they are made, in ordinary litigation between parties, in personal actions, the people will have ceased, to be their own rulers, having, to that extent, practically resigned their government, into the hands of that eminent tribunal. Nor is there, in this view, any assault upon the court, or the judges. It is a duty, from which they may not shrink, to decide cases properly brought before them; and it is no fault of theirs, if others seek to turn their decisions to political purposes.

One section of our country believes slavery is *right*, and ought to be extended, while the other believes it is *wrong*, and ought not to be extended. This is the only substantial dispute. The fugitive slave clause of the Constitution, and the law for the suppression of the foreign slave trade, are each as well enforced, perhaps, as any law can ever be in a community where the moral sense of the people imperfectly supports the law itself. The great body of the people abide by the dry legal obligation in both cases, and a few break over in each. This, I think, cannot be perfectly cured; and it would be worse in both cases *after* the separation of the sections, than before. The foreign slave trade, now imperfectly suppressed, would be ultimately revived without restriction, in one section; while fugitive slaves, now only partially surrendered, would not be surrendered at all, by the other.

Physically speaking, we cannot separate. We cannot remove our respective sections from each other, nor build an impassable wall between them. A husband and wife may be divorced, and go out of the presence, and beyond the reach of each other; but the different parts of our country cannot do this. They cannot but remain face to face; and intercourse, either amicable or hostile, must continue between them. Is it possible then to make that intercourse more advantageous, or more satisfactory, *after* separation than *before*? Can aliens make treaties easier than friends can make laws? Can treaties be more faithfully enforced between aliens, than laws can among friends? Suppose you go to war, you cannot fight always; and when, after much loss on both sides, and no gain on either, you cease fighting, the identical old questions, as to terms of intercourse, are again upon you.

This country, with its institutions, belongs to the people who inhabit it. Whenever they shall grow weary of the existing government, they can exercise their *constitutional* right of amending it, or their *revolutionary* right to dismember, or overthrow it. I can not be ignorant of the fact that many worthy, and patriotic citizens are desirous of having the national constitution amended. While I make no recommendation of amendments, I fully recognize the rightful authority of the people over the whole subject, to be exercised in either of the modes prescribed in the instrument itself; and I should, under existing circumstances, favor, rather than oppose, a fair oppertunity being afforded the people to act upon it.

I will venture to add that, to me, the convention mode seems preferable, in that it allows amendments to originate with the people themselves, instead of only permitting them to take, or reject, propositions, originated by others, not especially chosen for the purpose, and which might not be precisely such, as they would wish to either accept or refuse. I understand a proposed amendment to the Constitution—which amendment, however, I have not seen, has passed Congress, to the effect that the federal government, shall never interfere with the domestic institutions of the States, including that of persons held to service. To avoid misconstruction of what I have said, I depart from my purpose not to speak of particular amendments, so far as to say that, holding such a provision to now be implied constitutional law, I have no objection to its being made express, and irrevocable.

The Chief Magistrate derives all his authority from the people, and they have conferred none upon him to fix terms for the separation of the States. The people themselves can do this also if they choose; but the executive, as such, has nothing to do with it. His duty is to administer the present government, as it came to his hands, and to transmit it, unimpaired by him, to his successor.

Why should there not be a patient confidence in the ultimate justice of the people? Is there any better, or equal hope, in the world? In our present differences, is either party without faith of being in the right? If the Almighty Ruler of nations, with his eternal truth and justice, be on your side of the North, or on yours of the South, that truth, and that justice, will surely prevail, by the judgment of this great tribunal, the American people.

By the frame of the government under which we live, this same people have wisely given their public servants but little power for mischief; and have, with equal wisdom, provided for the return of that little to their own hands at very short intervals.

While the people retain their virtue, and vigilence, no administration, by any extreme of wickedness or folly, can very seriously injure the government, in the short space of four years.

My countrymen, one and all, think calmly and *well*, upon this whole subject. Nothing valuable can be lost by taking time. If there be an object to *hurry* any of you, in hot haste, to a step which you would never take *deliberately*, that object will be frustrated by taking time; but no good object can be frustrated by it. Such of you as are now dissatisfied, still have the old Constitution unimpaired, and, on the sensitive point, the laws of your own framing under it; while the new administration will have no immediate power, if it would, to change either. If it were admitted that you who are dissatisfied, hold the right side in the dispute, there still is no single good reason for precipitate action. Intelligence, patriotism, Christianity, and a firm reliance on Him, who has never yet forsaken this favored land, are still competent to adjust, in the best way, all our present difficulty.

In *your* hands, my dissatisfied fellow countrymen, and not in *mine*, is the momentous issue of civil war. The government will not assail *you*. You can have no conflict, without being yourselves the aggressors. You have no oath registered in Heaven to destroy the government, while *I* shall have the most solemn one to "preserve, protect and defend" it.

I am loth to close. We are not enemies, but friends. We must not be enemies. Though passion may have strained, it must not break our bonds of affection. The mystic chords of memory, streching from every battle-field, and patriot grave, to every living heart and hearthstone, all over this broad land, will yet swell the chorus of the Union, when again touched, as surely they will be, by the better angels of our nature.

Lincoln's first inauguration. Photograph by Benjamin French, March 4, 1861. *Courtesy of Library of Congress*

ADDRESS DELIVERED AT THE DEDICATION OF THE CEMETERY AT GETTYSBURG

Delivered November 19, 1863, in Gettysburg, Pennsylvania

Four score and seven years ago our fathers brought forth on this continent, a new nation, conceived in Liberty, and dedicated to the proposition that all men are created equal.

Now we are engaged in a great civil war, testing whether that nation, or any nation so conceived, and so dedicated, can long endure. We are met on a great battle-field of that war. We have come to dedicate a portion of that field, as a final resting place for those who here gave their lives, that that nation might live. It is altogether fitting and proper that we should do this.

But, in a larger sense, we can not dedicate—we can not consecrate—we can not hallow—this ground. The brave men, living and dead, who struggled here, have consecrated it, far above our poor power to add or detract. The world will little note, nor long remember, what we say here, but it can never forget what they did here. It is for us, the living, rather, to be dedicated here to the unfinished work which they who fought here, have, thus far, so nobly advanced. It is rather for us to be here dedicated to the great task remaining before us—that from these honored dead we take increased devotion to that cause for which they gave the last full measure of devotion—that we here highly resolve that these dead shall not have died in vain—that this nation, under God, shall have a new birth of freedom—and that, government of the people, by the people, for the people, shall not perish from the earth.

Lincoln at Gettysburg. Photograph by David Bachrach, November 19, 1863. *ALPLM*

SECOND INAUGURAL ADDRESS

Delivered March 4, 1865, U.S. Capitol, Washington, D.C.

At this second appearing to take the oath of the presidential office, there is less occasion for an extended address than there was at the first. Then a statement, somewhat in detail, of a course to be pursued, seemed fitting and proper. Now, at the expiration of four years, during which public declarations have been constantly called forth on every point and phase of the great contest which still absorbs the attention, and engrosses the enerergies [*sic*] of the nation, little that is new could be presented. The progress of our arms, upon which all else chiefly depends, is as well known to the public as to myself; and it is, I trust, reasonably satisfactory and encouraging to all. With high hope for the future, no prediction in regard to it is ventured.

On the occasion corresponding to this four years ago, all thoughts were anxiously directed to an impending civil-war. All dreaded it—all sought to avert it. While the inaugeral address was being delivered from this place, devoted altogether to *saving* the Union without war, insurgent agents were in the city seeking to *destroy* it without war—seeking to dissol[v]e the Union, and divide effects, by negotiation. Both parties deprecated war; but one of them would *make* war rather than let the nation survive; and the other would *accept* war rather than let it perish. And the war came.

One eighth of the whole population were colored slaves, not distributed generally over the Union, but localized in the Southern part of it. These slaves constituted a peculiar and powerful interest. All knew that this interest was, somehow, the cause of the war. To strengthen, perpetuate, and extend this interest was the object for which the insurgents would rend the Union, even by war; while the government claimed no right to do more than to restrict the territorial enlargement of it. Neither party expected for the war, the magnitude, or the duration, which it has already attained. Neither anticipated that the *cause* of the conflict might cease with, or even before, the conflict itself should cease. Each looked for an easier triumph, and a result less fundamental and astounding. Both read the same Bible, and pray to the same God; and each invokes His aid against the other. It may seem strange that any men should dare to ask a just God's assistance in wringing their bread from the sweat of other men's faces; but let us judge not that we be not judged. The prayers of both could not be answered; that of neither has been answered fully. The Almighty has His own purposes. "Woe unto the world because of offences! for it must needs be that offences come; but woe to that man by whom the offence cometh!" If we shall suppose that American Slavery is one of those offences which, in the providence of God, must needs come, but which, having continued through His appointed time, He now wills to remove, and that He gives to both North and South, this terrible war, as the woe due to those by whom the offence came, shall we discern therein any departure from those divine attributes which the believers in a Living God always ascribe to Him? Fondly do we hope—fervently do we pray—that this mighty scourge of war may speedily pass away. Yet, if God wills that it continue, until all the wealth piled by the bond-man's two hundred and fifty years of unrequited toil shall be sunk, and until every drop of blood drawn with the lash, shall be paid by another drawn with the sword, as was said three thousand years ago, so still it must be said "the judgments of the Lord, are true and righteous altogether."

With malice toward none; with charity for all; with firmness in the right, as God gives us to see the right, let us strive on to finish the work we are in; to bind up the nation's wounds; to care for him who shall have borne the battle, and for his widow, and his orphan—to do all which may achieve and cherish a just, and a lasting peace, among ourselves, and with all nations.

Lincoln delivering the Second Inaugural Address. Photograph by Alexander Gardner, March 4, 1865. *ALPLM*

THE SPEECH ON RECONSTRUCTION

Delivered April 11, 1865, White House Upstairs Window, Washington, D.C.

We meet this evening, not in sorrow, but in gladness of heart. The evacuation of Petersburg and Richmond, and the surrender of the principal insurgent army, give hope of a righteous and speedy peace whose joyous expression can not be restrained. In the midst of this, however, He, from Whom all blessings flow, must not be forgotten. A call for a national thanksgiving is being prepared, and will be duly promulgated. Nor must those whose harder part gives us the cause of rejoicing, be overlooked. Their honors must not be parcelled out with others. I myself, was near the front, and had the high pleasure of transmitting much of the good news to you; but no part of the honor, for plan or execution, is mine. To Gen. Grant, his skilful officers, and brave men, all belongs. The gallant Navy stood ready, but was not in reach to take active part.

By these recent successes the re-inauguration of the national authority—reconstruction—which has had a large share of thought from the first, is pressed much more closely upon our attention. It is fraught with great difficulty. Unlike the case of a war between independent nations, there is no authorized organ for us to treat with. No one man has authority to give up the rebellion for any other man. We simply must begin with, and mould from, disorganized and discordant elements. Nor is it a small additional embarrassment that we, the loyal people, differ among ourselves as to the mode, manner, and means of reconstruction.

As a general rule, I abstain from reading the reports of attacks upon myself, wishing not to be provoked by that to which I can not properly offer an answer. In spite of this precaution, however, it comes to my knowledge that I am much censured for some supposed agency in setting up, and seeking to sustain, the new State Government of Louisiana. In this I have done just so much as, and no more than, the public knows. In the Annual Message of Dec. 1863 and accompanying Proclamation, I presented a plan of re-construction (as the phrase goes) which, I promised, if adopted by any State, should be acceptable to, and sustained by, the Executive government of the nation. I distinctly stated that this was not the only plan which might possibly be acceptable; and I also distinctly protested that the Executive claimed no right to say when, or whether members should be admitted to seats in Congress from such States. This plan was, in advance, submitted to the then Cabinet, and distinctly approved by every member of it. One of them suggested that I should then, and in that connection, apply the Emancipation Proclamation to the theretofore excepted parts of Virginia and Louisiana; that I should drop the suggestion about apprenticeship for freed-people, and that I should omit the protest against my own power, in regard to the admission of members to Congress; but even he approved every part and parcel of the plan which has since been employed or touched by the action of Louisiana. The new constitution of Louisiana, declaring emancipation for the whole State, practically applies the Proclamation to the part previously excepted. It does not adopt apprenticeship for freed-people; and it is silent, as it could not well be otherwise, about the admission of members to Congress. So that, as it applies to Louisiana, every member of the Cabinet fully approved the plan. The Message went to Congress, and I received many commendations of the plan, written and verbal; and not a single objection to it, from any professed emancipationist, came to my knowledge, until after the news reached Washington that the people of Louisiana had begun to move in accordance with it. From about July 1862, I had corresponded with different persons, supposed to be interested, seeking a reconstruction of a State government for Louisiana. When the Message of 1863, with the plan before mentioned, reached New-Orleans, Gen. Banks wrote me that he was confident the people, with his military co-operation, would reconstruct, substantially on that plan. I wrote him, and some of them to try it; they tried it, and the result is known. Such only has been my agency in getting up the Louisiana government. As to sustaining it, my promise is out, as before stated. But, as bad promises are better broken than kept, I shall treat this as a bad promise, and break it, whenever I shall be convinced that keeping it is adverse to the public interest. But I have not yet been so convinced.

I have been shown a letter on this subject, supposed to be an able one, in which the writer expresses regret that my mind has not seemed to be definitely fixed on the question whether the seceded States, so called, are in the Union or out of it. It would perhaps, add astonishment to his regret, were he to learn that since I have found professed Union men endeavoring to make that question, I have *purposely* forborne any public expression upon it. As appears to me that question has not been, nor yet is, a practically material one, and that any discussion of it, while it thus remains practically immaterial, could have no effect other than the mischievous one of dividing our friends. As yet, whatever it may hereafter become, that question is bad, as the basis of a controversy, and good for nothing at all—a merely pernicious abstraction.

We all agree that the seceded States, so called, are out of their proper practical relation with the Union; and that the sole object of the government, civil and military, in regard to those States is to again get them into that proper practical relation. I believe it is not only possible, but in fact, easier, to do this, without deciding, or even considering, whether these states have even been out of the Union, than with it. Finding themselves safely at home, it would be utterly immaterial whether they had ever been abroad. Let us all join in doing the acts necessary to restoring the proper practical relations between these states and the Union; and each forever after, innocently indulge his own opinion whether, in doing the acts, he brought the States from without, into the Union, or only gave them proper assistance, they never having been out of it.

The amount of constituency, so to to [*sic*] speak, on which the new Louisiana government rests, would be more satisfactory to all, if it contained fifty, thirty, or even twenty thousand, instead of only about twelve thousand, as it does. It is also unsatisfactory to some that the elective franchise is not given to the colored man. I would myself prefer that it were now conferred on the very intelligent, and on those who serve our cause as soldiers. Still the question is not whether the Louisiana government, as it stands, is quite all that is desirable. The question is "Will it be wiser to take it as it is, and help to improve it; or to reject, and disperse it?" "Can Louisiana be brought into proper practical relation with the Union *sooner* by *sustaining*, or by *discarding* her new State Government?"

Some twelve thousand voters in the heretofore slave-state of Louisiana have sworn allegiance to the Union, assumed to be the rightful political power of the State, held elections, organized a State government, adopted a free-state constitution, giving the benefit of public schools equally to black and white, and empowering the Legislature to confer the elective franchise upon the colored man. Their Legislature has already voted to ratify the constitutional amendment recently passed by Congress, abolishing slavery throughout the nation. These twelve thousand persons are thus fully committed to the Union, and to perpetual freedom in the state—committed to the very things, and nearly all the things the nation wants—and they ask the nations recognition, and it's assistance to make good their committal. Now, if we reject, and spurn them, we do our utmost to disorganize and disperse them. We in effect say to the white men "You are worthless, or worse—we will neither help you, nor be helped by you." To the blacks we say "This cup of liberty which these, your old masters, hold to your lips, we will dash from you, and leave you to the chances of gathering the spilled and scattered contents in some vague and undefined when, where, and how." If this course, discouraging and paralyzing both white and black, has any tendency to bring Louisiana into proper practical relations with the Union, I have, so far, been unable to perceive it. If, on the contrary, we recognize, and sustain the new government of Louisiana the converse of all this is made true. We encourage the hearts, and nerve the arms of the twelve thousand to adhere to their work, and argue for it, and proselyte for it, and fight for it, and feed it, and grow it, and ripen it to a complete success. The colored man too, in seeing all united for him, is inspired with vigilance, and energy, and daring, to the same end. Grant that he desires the elective franchise, will he not attain it sooner by saving the already advanced steps toward it, than by running backward over them? Concede that the new government of Louisiana is only to what it should be as the egg is to the fowl, we shall sooner have the fowl by hatching the egg than by smashing it? Again, if we reject Louisiana, we also reject one vote in favor of the proposed amendment to the national constitution. To meet this proposition, it has been argued that no more than three fourths of those States which have not attempted secession are necessary to validly ratify the amendment. I do not commit myself against this, further than to say that such a ratification would be questionable, and sure to be persistently questioned; while a ratification by three fourths of all the States would be unquestioned and unquestionable.

I repeat the question. "Can Louisiana be brought into proper practical relation with the Union *sooner* by *sustaining* or by *discarding* her new State Government?"

What has been said of Louisiana will apply generally to other States. And yet so great peculiarities pertain to each state; and such important and sudden changes occur in the same state; and, withal, so new and unprecedented is the whole case, that no exclusive, and inflexible plan can safely be prescribed as to details and colatterals. Such exclusive, and inflexible plan, would surely become a new entanglement. Important principles may, and must, be inflexible.

In the present "*situation*" as the phrase goes, it may be my duty to make some new announcement to the people of the South. I am considering, and shall not fail to act, when satisfied that action will be proper.

Franchise. And Not This Man? Engraving from *Harper's Weekly*, August 5, 1865. *CHM*

EXHIBITION CHECKLIST

SECTION ONE: A HOUSE DIVIDED

Abraham Lincoln
Photograph by C. S. German, September
26, 1858
ALPLM

Speech of Hon. Abram Lincoln
Pamphlet
Sycamore, Illinois: O. P. Bassett, 1858
5.25" x 3.5"
ALPLM, Gift of Gov. Henry Horner, 1940

*Republican Principles: Speech of Hon.
Abraham Lincoln of Illinois, June 16,
1858*
Pamphlet
Printed by *The Evening Journal*, Albany,
NY, 1860
9" x 5.75"
ALPLM

Illinois State Capitol
Photograph, ca. 1858
Photographer unknown
ALPLM

Slave shackles
Maker unknown, ca. 1855
Iron
17.5" x 4.375" x 1"
CHM, X.1461

Cotton Pressing in Louisiana
Wood engraving from sketches by A. Hill
Ballou's Magazine, April 12, 1856
CHM, ICHi-34909

Field hoe head
W. Alyndon, England, ca. 1850
Iron
8.5" x 5" x 1.5"
CHM, Gift of Dr. John M. Pillsbury,
1923.84

Shoes worn by slave
Maker unknown, ca. 1860
Leather, wood, iron
3" x 4" x 12"
CHM, 1920.1734ab

Slave whip
Maker unknown, ca. 1850
Leather
49" length x 1.75" diameter
CHM, X.3427.2009

Twelve Years a Slave
Solomon Northup
Auburn, N.Y.: Derby & Miller, 1853
7.875" x 5.5" x 1.5" closed
ALPLM, acquired 1933

My Bondage and My Freedom
Frederick Douglass
New York and Auburn: Miller, Orton &
Mulligan, 1855
7.75" x 5.5" x 1.25" closed
ALPLM, acquired 1944

Sale of Slaves and Stock
Broadside, 1852
12.5" x 8"
CHM, Gift of Peter W. Rooney,
ICHi-22003

100 Dolls. Reward/Ran Away
Broadside, ca. 1855
12" x 9.5"
CHM, ICHi-22005

*Anti-Slavery/No Union With
Slaveholders!*
Broadside, ca. 1855
Printed by the Anti-Slavery Society,
Boston, Massachusetts
12.5" x 17"
CHM, ICHi-22020

William Lloyd Garrison
Photograph by C. Seaver, Jr., ca. 1858
CHM, ICHi-52584

John C. Calhoun
Photograph by Mathew Brady, ca. 1849
ALPLM

Henry Clay
Engraving by John Sartain, 1861, from a
painting by M. A. Root
ALPLM

Scene at the Lincoln-Douglas Debate
Engraving by Armand Welcker
First published in Francis F. Browne,
*The Every-Day Life of Abraham
Lincoln*. New York and St. Louis: N. D.
Thompson Publishing Co., 1886.
ALPLM

Portrait of Abraham Lincoln
Oil on canvas by William Camm, 1858
37.5" x 27"
ALPLM, acquired 1935

Portrait of Stephen A. Douglas
Oil on canvas by Louis A. Lussier, ca. 1858
36.5" x 28.25"
CHM, X.104

Note from Abraham Lincoln to Stephen
A. Douglas regarding debates
July 31, 1858
9.75" x 7.75"
CHM, Bequest of Lambert Tree,
ICHi-52011

Platform notes for the Jonesboro debate
Abraham Lincoln, September 15, 1858
7.5" x 5.5"
ALPLM, Gift of Caroline Catherine
Brown and Elizabeth Owsley
Brown, 1950

Grand Rally of the Lincoln Men of Old Tazewell!
Broadside
Printed by Pickett & Dowdell, Pekin, Illinois, 1858
33" x 29.75"
ALPLM

Political Debates between Hon. Abraham Lincoln and Hon. Stephen A. Douglas in the Celebrated Campaign of 1858, in Illinois
Inscribed by Lincoln to Abraham Jonas
Columbus, Ohio: Follett & Foster, 1860
13.5" x 9.5" x 3" (open)
ALPLM, Gift of Frederick B. Wells, 1947

SECTION TWO: THE FIRST INAUGURAL ADDRESS

Abraham Lincoln
Photograph by C. S. German, February 9, 1861
ALPLM, Gift of A. C. Goodyear, 1954

Printer's galleys of Abraham Lincoln's First Inaugural Address
Springfield, Ill.: Baker & Bailhache, 1861
14.5" x 9" (8 leaves)
ALPLM, acquired 1961

Inkwell used by Abraham Lincoln to write the First Inaugural Address
Maker unknown, ca. 1860
Wood and metal
2.25" high x 4.75" diameter
ALPLM

Lincoln's First Inauguration
Photograph by Benjamin French, March 4, 1861
ALPLM

Free Homes for Free Men / Lincoln & Hamlin
Campaign banner, artist unknown, 1860
Oil on silk
60" x 52"
ALPLM, acquired 1941

Bust of Abraham Lincoln
Leonard Volk, 1860
Plaster
30" x 17" x 11"
ALPLM

Lincoln campaign coin
Maker unknown, 1860
Brass
.875" diameter
ALPLM

Lincoln campaign badge
Satin & Paper Badge Depot, Philadelphia, 1860
Paper
7.687" x 3.125"
ALPLM

Eagle figure from Wide Awakes campaign torch
Maker unknown, 1860 or 1864
Copper alloy
9.75" x 9" x 3"
ALPLM

Campaign rally in front of Lincoln's Springfield home
Photograph by William A. Shaw, August 8, 1860
ALPLM, Gift of A. C. Goodyear, 1954

Lives and Speeches of Abraham Lincoln and Hannibal Hamlin
William Dean Howells
With pencil corrections by Lincoln through page ninety-four
Columbus, Ohio: Follett & Foster, 1860
8" x 9.5" open; 8" x 6" closed
ALPLM, Gift of Gov. Henry Horner, 1940

Republican Mass Meeting
Broadside
Printed by Journal Oscillator Press, Ithaca, NY, 1860
18" x 6.5"
ALPLM

The Union Is Dissolved
Broadside
Printed by *The Charleston Mercury*, December 20, 1860
22.75" x 12.625"
ALPLM

Jefferson Davis
Photograph by Mathew Brady, ca. 1860
ALPLM

Alexander Stephens
Photograph by Mathew Brady, ca. 1860
ALPLM

President and Cabinet
Engraving by J. C. Buttre, 1862
12" x 9.5"
ALPL Foundation / Taper Collection, 2007

President Lincoln with John Nicolay and John Hay
Photograph by Alexander Gardner, November 8, 1863
ALPLM

The Railsplitter
Oil on canvas by Chambers (first name unknown), 1860
102.75" x 84.5"
CHM, Gift of Miss Maibelle Heikes Justice, 1917.15

Abraham Lincoln
Photograph by William Marsh, May 20, 1860
CHM, ICHi-53537

John C. Breckinridge
Photograph by Mathew Brady, 1860
CHM, ICHi-52468

John Bell
Photograph by Mathew Brady, c. 1860
CHM, ICHi-52467

Stephen A. Douglas
Photograph by Case & Getchell, c. 1860
CHM, ICHi-22013

Carriage used by the Lincoln Family in Washington, DC
J. B. Brewster & Co., New York, 1861
Painted wood, iron, wool felt, glass
81" x 72" x 156"
CHM, 1920.238

Queen Victoria of Great Britain
Photograph by Alexander Bassano, 1882
CHM, ICHi-69819

Napoleon III of France
Photographer unknown, ca. 1870
CHM, IChi-53705

President Benito Juarez of Mexico
Lithograph portrait, ca. 1865
CHM, IChi-52075

Emperor Franz-Josef of Austria
Photographer unknown, ca. 1915
CHM, IChi-69820

William Wallace Lincoln
Watercolor on paper, 1862, artist
    unknown, from photograph by Mathew
    Brady, 1861
27.5" x 22.5"
ALPLM, Gift of Robert Todd Lincoln
    Beckwith, 1977

Mary Lincoln in strawberry dress
Photograph by Mathew Brady, 1861
ALPLM

Letter from Mary Lincoln inviting Ozias
    M. Hatch to dinner at the Executive
    Mansion
October 1, 1862
6.75" x 4.37"
ALPLM, Gift of Hatch Family heirs, 1990

Letter seal used by Mary Lincoln
Maker unknown, 1861
3.75" x 1.187"
ALPLM, Gift of Robert Todd Lincoln
    Beckwith, 1976

The Last Days of Pompeii (2 vols.)
Signed and dated by Mary Lincoln, 1864
Written by Edward Bulwer-Lytton
Philadelphia: J. B. Lippincott, 1860
7.37" x 5" x 1.12" per volume, closed
ALPL Foundation / Taper Collection, 2007

Robert Todd Lincoln
Photographer unknown, 1861
ALPLM

Manuscript of a telegram from R. T.
    Lincoln to A. Lincoln
July 17, 1861
8" x 5.25"
ALPLM, acquired in 1954

Album of photographs taken at Harvard
    College
Compiled by Robert Lincoln, ca.
    1861–1864
6.25" x 9.75" x 2.25"
ALPLM, Gift of Robert Todd Lincoln
    Beckwith, 1976

Alice Huntington
Professor of Rhetoric James Jennison
Harvard Hall
Photographs from Robert Lincoln's
    Harvard album, ca. 1863
ALPLM, Gifts of Robert Todd Lincoln
    Beckwith, 1976

William Wallace Lincoln, 1861
Photograph by Mathew Brady
ALPLM

Letter from Willie Lincoln to
    Henry Remann
May 25, 1861
8" x 5.25"
ALPLM, Gift of Mary Edwards
    Brown, 1955

Funeral address for Willie Lincoln
Rev. Phineas D. Gurley, February 24, 1862
Privately printed
9" x 7.25"
ALPLM, acquired in 1935

Walking cane presented to Rev.
    Phineas D. Gurley by Abraham and
    Mary Lincoln
Maker unknown, 1862
Ebony and gold
36" length
CHM, Gift of Mrs. Joseph Cudahy,
    1952.238

Tad Lincoln
Hand-tinted photograph
Attributed to Mathew Brady, July 1861
ALPLM, Gift of the Robert E. Myers, Jr.,
    Trust, 2010

Patent-model cannon presented by Capt. J.
    A. Dahlgren to Tad Lincoln
Maker unknown, 1862
Brass and wood
5.75" x 5.75" x 12.75"
ALPLM, acquired 1941

Note from Abraham Lincoln to Capt. J. A.
    Dahlgren
October 14, 1862
3.12" x 1.87"
ALPLM, acquired in 1941

Note from Abraham Lincoln
    recommending William Johnson
October 24, 1862
3.25" x 2"
ALPLM, acquired 1940

Check for five dollars from Abraham
    Lincoln to William Johnson
March 11, 1862
3" x 7.5"
ALPLM, acquired in 1941

Elizabeth Keckly
Photographer unknown, ca. 1858,
    reissued by Paul Tralles, 1868
ALPLM, acquired in 2011

Spoon reportedly used by Abraham
    Lincoln on April 14, 1865
Collected by Elizabeth Keckly
Sterling silver, 7.25"
ALPLM, Gift of Margaret Kirkpatrick,
    1970

Note stating that Lincoln used the spoon
Written by Elizabeth Keckly,
    April 16, 1865
3" x 8"
ALPLM, Gift of Margaret Kirkpatrick,
    1970

SECTION THREE: THE GETTYSBURG ADDRESS

Abraham Lincoln
Photograph by Alexander Gardner,
    November 8, 1863
ALPLM, Gift of A. C. Goodyear, 1954

The Gettysburg Address, November 1863
Original copy written by Abraham
    Lincoln in February 1864
22.5" x 30.5"
ALPLM, Gift of Marshall Field III and
    the Children of Illinois, 1944

Lincoln at Gettysburg
Photograph by David Bachrach,
    November 19, 1863
ALPLM

*Programme of Arrangements and Order
    of Exercises for the Inauguration of the
    National Cemetery at Gettysburg*
Printed by Gideon & Pearson,
    Washington DC
8.66" x 11.02"
ALPLM

*Bombardment of Fort Sumter,
    Charleston Harbor*
Lithograph by Currier & Ives, 1861
CHM, ICHi-22041

Map of the Southern States
Published in *Harper's Weekly*,
    November 1861
33" x 23"
CHM, Gift of Seymour Morris,
    ICHi-52572

*Jeff. Davis Going to War/Jeff. Davis
    Returns from War*
Cartoon by E. Rogers, 1861
6.5" x 5"
ALPLM

Hibernia Greens in the Irish Brigade
Union army recruitment broadside, 1862
21" x 28"
ALPLM

To Arms, Freemen, To Arms
Union army recruitment broadside, 1862
26" x 21"
ALPLM

Enlist in Dick Oglesby's Old Regiment
Union army recruitment broadside, 1862
24" x 16.5"
ALPLM

Union army infantryman's jacket
Wool with brass buttons
Made by John Martin, New York, 1861–62
23" x 17.5"
CHM, X.1545.1990

Union army drum used by the 9th
    Vermont Infantry, 1861–65
Wood, skin, rope, leather, brass
15.5" x 16.625"
CHM, 1920.691

.58 caliber percussion rifle musket
National Armory, Springfield,
    Massachusetts
U.S. Model 1861, made 1864
Walnut and steel
38" length
CHM, 1920.1386

.577 caliber percussion carbine
Royal Small Arms Factory, Enfield,
    England, 1862
Walnut and steel
36.5" length
CHM, 1920.1350

The Council of War
Sculpture by John Rogers, 1867
Bronze over plaster
24.5" x 18" x 17"
ALPL Foundation / Taper Collection, 2007

President's War Order No. 3
Abraham Lincoln, March 11, 1862
13.75" x 7.75"
ALPLM, acquired in 1941

Major General George B. McClellan
Photograph by Case & Getchel, 1862
ALPLM

Camp Scene on the Pamunkey River
Photograph by Taylor and Huntington,
    May 1862
CHM, ICHi-22156

General Joseph E. Johnston
Photographer unknown, ca. 1862
ALPLM

General Robert E. Lee
Photograph by Julian Vannerson, 1863
CHM, ICHi-52539

Charles Sumner
Photographer unknown, 1860
ALPLM, Gift of A. C. Goodyear, 1954

Horace Greeley
Photograph by Sarony & Co., New York,
    ca. 1860
ALPLM

Printed copy of the Emancipation
    Proclamation
Signed by Abraham Lincoln, William H.
    Seward, and John Nicolay, 1863
27.5" x 20"
ALPLM, Gift of Jesse J. Ricks, 1937

Pen used by Lincoln to sign printed copies
    of the Emancipation Proclamation
Made by C. Parker, 1860
5.75"
ALPLM, acquired in 1954

Freedom to Slaves!
Broadside, 1863
11" x 12"
ALPLM

Emancipation Proclamation
Pamphlet, 1863
2.25" x 3.25"
ALPL Foundation / Taper Collection, 2007

Writing the Emancipation Proclamation
Cartoon by Adalbert J. Volck, 1863
10.25" x 8" [CWE #3]
ALPLM, Gift of Congressman Morton D.
    Hall, 1933

Come and Join Us Brothers
Union army recruitment broadside
Printed by P. S. Duval & Son,
    Philadelphia, 1863
13.75" x 18"
CHM, ICHi-22051

Letter from Abraham Lincoln to
    Gen. Ulysses S. Grant at Vicksburg
    regarding black troops
August 9, 1863
9.75" x 9"
CHM, ICHi-52416 (recto), 52417 (verso)

African American Union army soldiers
Photographer unknown, ca. 1863
CHM, ICHi-22172, 22117

Scrimshaw portrait of African American
    Union army soldier
Maker unknown, ca. 1863
Inscribed whale tooth
5.5" x 2"
CHM, Gift of Mrs. Charles B. Pike,
    1942.67b

SECTION FOUR: THE SECOND INAUGURAL ADDRESS

Abraham Lincoln
Photograph by Alexander Gardner,
    February 5, 1865
ALPLM

Letter from Abraham Lincoln to Amanda
    Hall with passage from Second
    Inaugural Address
March 20, 1865
8" x 8.5"
ALPLM, acquired in 1976

View of Lincoln delivering the Second
    Inaugural Address
Photograph by Alexander Gardner,
    March 4, 1865
ALPLM

*Rebel Works in front of Atlanta, Georgia,
    No. 1*
Photograph by George Barnard, summer
    1864
CHM, ICHi-07822

Lincoln campaign lantern
Maker unknown, 1864
Glass and metal
8.5" x 5" x 5"
ALPLM, acquired in 1989

Lincoln-Johnson campaign ribbon
Maker unknown, 1864
Silk with colored inks
4.125" x 2.375"
ALPLM, acquired in 2010

Lincoln effigy doll
Maker unknown, ca. 1864
Cloth, sticks, buttons, hair, paper mask
10.5" x 3.5" x 3"
ALPL Foundation / Taper Collection, 2007

Commemorative copy of the Thirteenth
    Amendment
Signed by Lincoln and members of
    Congress, February 1, 1865
Ink on vellum
19.75" x 15.75"
ALPLM, acquired in 1941

Scene in the House, January 31, 1865
Woodcut from *Harper's Weekly*, February
    18, 1865
ALPLM

Photograph album
Compiled by Senator James Harlan, 1865
Leather, porcelain, metal, gilt-stamping
11" x 9.5" x 2.75"
ALPLM, Gift of Robert Todd Lincoln
    Beckwith, 1976

Lincoln's Drive through Richmond
Oil on canvas by Dennis Malone Carter,
    1867
45" x 68"
CHM, Gift of Mr. Philip K. Wrigley,
    1955.398

Major General Ulysses S. Grant
Photographer unknown, fall 1863
ALPLM, Gift of A. C. Goodyear, 1954

The Ruins of Richmond
Photograph by A. J. Russell, April 1865
CHM, ICHi-22116

Lincoln's last order to U. S. Grant
April 7, 1865
9.875" x 4"
CHM, ICHi-30836

SECTION FIVE: THE SPEECH ON RECONSTRUCTION

Abraham Lincoln
Photograph by Henry Warren,
    March 6, 1865
ALPLM

Lincoln's Last Public Address
April 11, 1865
Complete Works of Abraham Lincoln
Edited by John Nicolay and John Hay
New York: Francis D. Tandy Co., 1905
9.25" x 12" x 3" (open)
ALPLM

Franchise. And Not This Man?
Engraving from *Harper's Weekly*,
    August 5, 1865
CHM, ICHI-36864

Bed in which Abraham Lincoln died
Maker unknown, ca. 1860
Walnut
46.125" height x 53.75" width
    x 78.5 " length
CHM, 1920.249

The Last Hours of Lincoln
Oil on canvas by Alonzo Chappel, 1868
    (reproduction)
CHM, ICHI-52425

Playbill from Ford's Theatre
April 14, 1865
Printed by H. Polkinhorn & Co.,
    Washington, DC
47" x 16"
ALPL Foundation / Taper Collection, 2007

Ford's Theatre, 1865
Photographer unknown
ALPLM, Gift of A. C. Goodyear, 1954

The Assassination of President Lincoln
Color print
Printed by Pharazyn, Philadelphia, 1865
10.25" x 14"
ALPLM

The Last Hours of Lincoln
Print by John B. Bachelder, 1868
    (never published)
10" x 12"
ALPLM, Gift of LaSalle National
    Bank, 2004

Lincoln's blood-stained gloves
Maker unknown, ca. 1865
Kid leather
10" x 5"
ALPL Foundation / Taper Collection, 2007

Piece of Lincoln's shirt pinned to letter
Letter from Mose Sandford to John
    Beatty, April 17, 1865
Shirt: 1" x 3" (approximately); Letter:
    9.75" x 7.75"
ALPL Foundation / Taper Collection, 2007

Framed collection of Lincoln
    assassination relics: fragments
    of curtain and curtain tie from
    presidential box at Ford's Theatre, carte
    de visite of Lincoln family and envelope
    by George Sizer
13.9" x 9" x 1"
Courtesy of a Private Collection

$100,000 Reward!
Wanted poster for John Wilkes Booth,
    John Surratt, and David Herold
Printed by War Department, Washington,
    DC, April 20, 1865
26.5" x 15" with three CDVs, each 4" x 2.5"
ALPL Foundation / Taper Collection, 2007

Booth & His Associates
Composite image of Lincoln assassination
    conspirators
Maker unknown, 1865
4" x 2.5"
ALPL Foundation / Taper Collection, 2007

Mrs. Mary E. Surratt
Photographer unknown, ca. 1864
ALPLM

John Surratt
Photographer unknown, ca. 1866
ALPLM

*The Execution of Mrs. Surratt and the
    Lincoln Assassination Conspirators*
Photograph by Alexander Gardner,
    July 7, 1865
CHM, ICHi-52370

Playbill for John Wilkes Booth as
    MacBeth
Printed by J.H. & F.F. Farwell Ptg.,
    Boston, 1863
18.5" x 6.125"
ALPL Foundation / Taper Collection, 2007

Playbill for John Wilkes Booth
    as Raphael, the Sculptor in
    The Marble Heart
Printed by F.A. Searle, Ptr, Boston, 1864
14.37" x 5.75"
ALPL Foundation / Taper Collection, 2007

Carte-de-visite of John Wilkes Booth
Given by Booth to Isabel Sumner
Case & Getchell, Boston, 1862
4" x 2.5"
ALPL Foundation / Taper Collection, 2007

Letter from John Wilkes Booth to
    Isabel Sumner
June 17, 1864
8" x 10.5"
ALPL Foundation / Taper Collection, 2007

Ring given by John Wilkes Booth to
    Isabel Sumner
Inscribed on inside: "J.W.B. to I.S."
Maker unknown, 1864
Gold, silver, pearl: .787" diameter
ALPL Foundation / Taper Collection, 2007

The Spectre Bridegroom
Play script used and marked by John
    Wilkes Booth, 1858
5.75" x 4"
ALPL Foundation / Taper Collection, 2007

Edwin Booth
Photographer unknown, 1879
6.5" x 4.25"
ALPL Foundation / Taper Collection, 2007

Map of the Lincoln Funeral Train Route
Rand, McNally, Chicago, 1872
4.5" x 10.5"
ALPLM

Lincoln's funeral train in Cleveland
Photographer unknown, April 28, 1865
ALPL Foundation / Taper Collection, 2007

Timetable for Lincoln's funeral train from
    Cleveland to Columbus
Printed by Sanford & Hayward,
    Cleveland, 1865
10.875" x 6"
ALPL Foundation / Taper Collection, 2007

Lincoln funeral rosette
Maker unknown, 1865
Various fabrics
4" x 4"
ALPLM, Gift of Dorothy R. Willard, 1964

Lincoln funeral rosette
Maker unknown, 1865
Various fabrics, including black crepe
16" x 3"
ALPL Foundation / Taper Collection, 2007

Lincoln's entombment at Oak Ridge
    Cemetery, Springfield
Photograph by Ridgway Glover of
    Philadelphia, May 4, 1865
ALPLM

*Funeral Address Delivered at the Burial of
    President Lincoln*
Rev. Matthew Simpson, D.D.
Printer unknown, 1865
7.25" x 5"
ALPLM, Gift of Gov. Henry Horner, 1940

Programme of Reception
Broadside
Springfield: Committee on
    Reception, 1865
7.87" x 5"
ALPLM

Formal condolence to Mrs. Lincoln
Borough of Oldham, England:
    calligrapher unknown, 1865
Ink on vellum
22" x 18"
ALPLM

EPILOGUE: FROM FREEDOM TO EQUALITY

The Fifteenth Amendment
Color lithograph
New York: Thomas Kelly, 1870
11" x 14"
ALPLM

*The Shackle Broken – By the Genius
    of Freedom*
Color lithograph
Baltimore: E. Sachs & Co., 1874
21.5" x 20.5"
CHM, ICHi-22125

Letter from Abraham Lincoln to Maj.
    Gen. Nathaniel P. Banks regarding
    education for young blacks
August 8, 1863
9.75" x 7.75"
ALPLM, acquired in 1939

Parlor Monuments to the Illustrious Dead
Building blocks of wood and paper
New York: Oakley & Mason, 1865
16" x 6.75" x 1.12" in this formation
ALPLM, acquired 1946

*National Half Century Anniversary
    Exposition and the Lincoln Jubilee*
Broadside, 1915
Printed by The Clinton Co., Chicago
44" x 28"
ALPLM

Souvenir doorknocker, "A House Divided
    against Itself Cannot Stand"
Maker unknown, ca. 1958
Brass
4" x 2.75"
ALPLM

*A House Divided against Itself Cannot
    Stand*
Introduction by Douglas C. McMurtrie
Chicago: Black Cat Press, 1936
9.5" x 13"
ALPLM, acquired 1936

Maquette for the Lincoln Memorial
Daniel Chester French, 1909
Plaster
34" x 24" x 14"
ALPLM, Gift of Illinois Benedictine
    College, 2006

Postcard, image of *Lincoln at the
    Crossroads of Decision* at Lincoln's New
    Salem
Avard Fairbanks, sculptor, 1954
Jumbo postcard printed in Berrien
    Springs, Mich.: Freeman Studios
9" x 6"
ALPLM

Lincoln Inaugural Centennial, 1861–1961
Album cover for long-play record,
    33 1/3 rpm
New York: Gold Star Recordings, Inc.,
    1961
12.25" x 12.25"
ALPLM, acquired 1961

Coffee mug with motto "Shall Not Perish"
    for *U.S.S. Abraham Lincoln*
Clay-based china
Westford, Mass.: Mil-Art China Co., 1989
3.94" diameter
ALPLM

Gettysburg Address T-shirt
cotton
24" x 30" unfolded
Honduras: Gildan Activewear, 2009
ALPLM

Amazon Kindle Fire HD 7"
    Wi-Fi® Tablet, 8GB
2014
7.5" x 5" x .4"
ALPLM

FOR FURTHER READING

Approximately 18,000 titles have been written on Lincoln over the last 175 years. The following list offers some of the best recent works that focus on Lincoln's key writings of 1858–1865. Readers are welcome to ask at the Abraham Lincoln Presidential Library and Museum or the Chicago History Museum for further recommendations or works more focused on any topic.
–Olivia Mahoney, CHM, and James Cornelius, ALPLM

Basler, Roy P., et al., eds. *Collected Works of Abraham Lincoln*. 8 vols. New Brunswick, NJ: Rutgers University Press for the Abraham Lincoln Association, 1953–55; online since 2006 at http://quod.lib.umich.edu/l/lincoln/

Boritt, Gabor. *The Gettysburg Gospel*. New York: Simon & Schuster, 2006.

Burlingame, Michael. *Abraham Lincoln: A Life*. 2 vols. Baltimore, MD: Johns Hopkins University Press, 2008.

Carwardine, Richard. *Lincoln: A Life of Purpose and Power*. New York: Knopf, 2006.

Cox, LaWanda. *Lincoln and Black Freedom*. Columbia: University of South Carolina Press, 1981.

Donald, David Herbert. *Lincoln*. New York: Simon & Schuster, 1995.

Fehrenbacher, Don E., ed. *Abraham Lincoln: Speeches and Writings*. 2 vols. New York: Library of America, 1989.

Foner, Eric, and Olivia Mahoney. *A House Divided: America in the Age of Lincoln*. Chicago: Chicago Historical Society; New York: W.W. Norton & Co., 1990.

Foner, Eric. *The Fiery Trial: Abraham Lincoln and American Slavery*. New York: W. W. Norton & Co., 2010.

Guelzo, Allen C. *Lincoln and Douglas: The Debates that Defined America*. New York: Simon & Schuster, 2008.

Holzer, Harold, Edna Greene Medford, and Frank J. Williams. Foreword by John Hope Franklin. *The Emancipation Proclamation: Three Views (Social, Political, Iconographic)*. Baton Rouge: Louisiana State University Press, 2006.

Mahoney, Olivia. "The Fiery Trial: Abraham Lincoln and the Civil War." http://publications.newberry.org/lincoln/fierytrial/, 2009.

McPherson, James. *Battle Cry of Freedom*. New York: Oxford University Press, 1988.

Paludan, Phillip Shaw. *The Presidency of Abraham Lincoln*. Lawrence: University Press of Kansas, 1994.

Peatman, Jared. *The Long Shadow of Lincoln's Gettysburg Address*. Carbondale: Southern Illinois University Press, 2013.

Vorenberg, Michael. *Final Freedom: The Civil War, the Abolition of Slavery, and the Thirteenth Amendment*. New York: Cambridge University Press, 2001.

White, Ronald C. *The Eloquent President*. New York: Random House, 2005.

Wilson, Douglas L. *Lincoln's Sword: The Presidency and the Power of Words*. New York: Knopf, 2006.

FOR YOUNGER READERS

Grades 7–12
Gregory, Josh. *The Gettysburg Address*. New York: Scholastic, Inc., 2014.

Harris, Laurie Lanzen. *How to Analyze the Works of Abraham Lincoln*. Minneapolis: ABDO Publishing, 2013.

Grades 3–6
Armentrout, David and Patricia Armentrout. *The Gettysburg Address* and *El Discurso de Gettysburg*. [separate English and Spanish editions] Vero Beach, FL: Rourke Publishing, 2006.

Harness, Cheryl. *Abe Lincoln Goes to Washington*. Washington, DC: National Geographic Society, 1997.